WHEN THE HEAVENS FROWNED

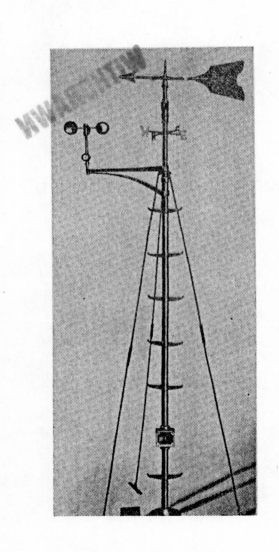

WHEN THE HEAVENS FROWNED

By

Dr. Joseph L. Cline

Maligned, cussed, discussed and much beloved Texas weather man.

AN AUTOBIOGRAPHY

A
FIREBIRD
PRESS
BOOK

Gretna 2000

Manufactured in the United States of America
Published by Pelican Publishing Company, Inc.
1000 Burmaster Street, Gretna, Louisiana 70053

DEDICATED

TO

MY WIFE

ULA JACKSON CLINE

Whose faith upheld me
Whose wisdom guided me
Whose love inspired me

CONTENTS

ILLUSTRATIONS

BIOGRAPHICAL DIRECTORY OF
AMERICAN MEN OF SCIENCE

Cline, Dr. Joseph L(eander), U. S. Weather Bureau Office, Dallas, Texas. *Meteorology*. Madisonville, Tenn, Sept. 20, 70. B.S., Hiwassee Col, 90; A.M., Ph.D, Add-Ran Univ. Teacher, pub. schs; asst. observer, U. S. *Weather Bur*, 92-00, observer and local forecaster, Texas, and director sect, P. R, 00-01, *meteorologist in charge office, Dallas*, 13- Lecturer, high and nor. schs, Texas. Rep, U. S. Weather Bur. meeting for flood control and conservation in Texas. Sig. C, U.S.A. A.A; Meteorol. Soc; Texas Forestry Asn. Climatology; weather forecasting; agriculture; climate of Texas in its relation to the cultivation of winter vegetables, tropical fruits, apples and olives; frost protection.

The name of Joseph Leander Cline appears in the *International Blue Book* (*Who's Who in The World*), a biographical dictionary of the World's Notable Living Men and Women, printed in English, French, German, Spanish, Italian, and other languages, 1939-1940.

UNITED STATES DEPARTMENT OF COMMERCE
WEATHER BUREAU
Washington, 25

November 27, 1944

Mr. Joseph L. Cline, B.Sc., A.M., Ph.D.,
231 W. 12th Street,
Dallas, Texas

Dear Mr. Cline:

It was a pleasure to have your letter of November 20 about the card "LOOK-READ" which we recently reprinted in *Topics*. We had no idea of its source and I was glad to have it identified.

You requested authority to reproduce the item as published in *Topics and Personnel*, in your forthcoming autobiography. We think that would be highly appropriate and accordingly this signifies the Bureau's permission. We shall be very interested in seeing a copy of your book when it comes out.

I am circulating your letter among Project Leaders here who know you. We are always happy to hear from members of the Weather Bureau who have completed long years of service and who retain their interest in the Bureau and its affairs during their period of retirement.

With best wishes and personal regards,

Sincerely yours,

F. W. Reichelderfer,
Chief of Bureau.

A LEGEND FROM THE PAST

· Recently a 3x5 card, somewhat yellowed with age, and carrying no identification other than the union label of the Allied Printing Trades Council, Dallas, Texas, appeared on the desk of the Chief of Bureau. It carried the following text:

LOOK-READ

The science of meteorology is not perfect, but is about as perfect as the science of medicine, and other closely related sciences. Errors in medicine are buried, but an imperfect forecast is advertised; as a result, one failure in forecasting is noticed more than a dozen perfect and successful predictions. There are many who comment on warnings, as not being verified, when they do not know whereof they speak. It is useless to argue with people who believe and follow fakers, or those who listen to street rumors and misrepresentations, and do not take the trouble or time to obtain correct information. Since the science of meteorology is not perfect, one should not even expect all reliable forecasts to be verified; however, warnings are often verified when people, who go by their feelings or by imperfect instruments, do not think so. Remember, you are not full of mercury; therefore you can not be a walking barometer or thermometer.

The following reference is made on page 392 of *Weather Bureau Topics and Personnel*, January, 1945:

AUTHOR IDENTIFIED

In the November issue of *Topics and Personnel*, a statement taken from an unidentified card was reprinted under the heading "A LEGEND FROM THE PAST." Since the item appeared we have a letter from Dr. Joseph L. Cline, formerly official in charge Dallas, now retired, informing us that he wrote the statement and published it more than twenty years ago. We are glad to identify the author.

INTRODUCTION

Dr. Joseph Leander Cline is one of the truly colorful personalities of the most colorful region—the southwestern United States. His character, actions, and life combine as an example of usefulness, ruggedness, and energy that has exerted a powerful influence in many directions. Younger men, who have worked under him in various posts of the United States Weather Bureau, have marvelled at this untiring machine of a man who has never run down. "Doc" Cline, as he is affectionately known to thousands of Texans, still maintains his activity, although he is well past seventy and retired as dean of southwestern weathermen. Throughout his life, he has pursued his calm and unswerving course, concealing the innate gentleness of his disposition beneath a tough and hardy exterior. He is a man in whom is united, to an almost unbelievable degree, the litheness of a greyhound with the strength and sagacity of a bulldog.

He earned the right to place the title "Doctor" before his name by taking his Ph.D. degree at Add-Ran University, an institution of learning in Waco, Texas. He is a man who has known tragedy, although his appearance belies it—a tall, lean, precise figure, with twinkling eyes that had developed, in his later years, a suggestion of squint, the latter possibly caused by gazing at the sun and skies for so long.

Merely his experience in the Galveston hurricane of 1900, a disaster comparable in these parts to the San Francisco Earthquake, the Johnstown Flood, or the Chicago Fire, reveals him as an intrepid figure, who, single-handed, performed Herculean feats in warning the people until he could no longer be of use in sticking to his post. He was then free to battle all that fateful night for his own life and the lives of members of his family.

This and other experiences would have furnished a rich backlog for a lifetime of anecdotes and yarns, but Dr. Cline, although a fluent talker when not on his beloved job, lived on in the present, and still does.

The weather of Texas, with its influence on human life and property, was his consuming passion, second only to the love that he had for his family and home. Despite the Mark Twain thesis that nobody ever does anything about the weather, Dr. Cline did all that anyone could in gauging its probable climatic effect upon crops and driving his sound theories home by means of lectures and writings. His papers on the cultivation of winter vegetables and seasonal fruits on the Texas Coast, the protection of crops against the "northers" that move like blue lightning several times each winter out of the Rockies, and on what might be expected from the climates in the areas of posts that he held, were hailed by growers, business men, and scientists alike as definite milestones in the rapid economic and agricultural progress of the state.

"Texas weather" is a phrase that sets this state apart, as does the vastness of its area. The saying is trite that nobody but a stranger or a fool ever tries to predict it. Dr. Cline not only tackled the often thankless job of forecasting the sudden changes or the long dry or wet, cold or warm periods, but did it right 95 per cent of the time, according to Bureau records. He roped and tied the ornery meteorological mustang, and was at his busiest—and therefore his happiest— when the public needed him to tell it how high the waters would rise, how cold the impending norther would be, or how dangerous the blizzard would become to livestock or to the under-sheltered poor.

In the middle of some soul-scorching heat wave, Dr. Cline defended the weather. It was always "Pretty warm, but not so bad as such-and-such a year." If cold, it was, "Right chilly last night, but after all, in nineteen so-and-so, it went down to umpty degrees below." Or again, he would remark,

"Yes, it's pretty dry, but it's got thirty-six days yet to go without rain, to establish a new record." Dr. Cline, as a close observer of the weather throughout the years, was not greatly moved by the minor variations of drought or storm. He never admitted the truth about the stranger and fool adage. He always said, "Nature is never so bad but what she can become worse," or, "We can always expect slight to severe changes in climate."

From sturdy and worthy stock, sprang Joseph Leander Cline, farmer, teacher, writer and scientist, whose feet as a youth were destined to carry him far from his own green Tennessee foothills to the interesting and sometimes dramatic career which awaited him. He was equipped with eye and brain alert to see and to achieve the success which came to him in his various fields, through days divided between happiness and sorrow, sunshine and hurricane winds. His hands were strong to carve for their owner a niche of his own in the world that grew troubled as he grew older, a world which he was to live to see shaken by tumult and by strife, by international intrigues and disputes, and finally by the terrific impact of global war.

Dr. Cline knows that these things have happened and believes that they will happen again. He has seen the plow turn in the earth and a seed planted. A tree, he observes, is felled to the ground and a house is built from its wood. Steady in his meteorological knowledge of those eternal elements, the sun, clouds, winds, and rain, he holds that a thought born and transferred to a piece of paper by the scientific mind may well outlast the results of many wars, in its significance to the growth of civilization and the impetus by which a great nation swings steadily forward.

—Ross T. Fitzgerald

THE CLINE ANCESTRY

The immediate ancestors of the American Clines settled in New Amsterdam and were of Dutch (Holland) extraction. The first census of Pennsylvania in 1790 showed several families bearing the surname of Cline, with such given names as John, Jacob, William and George, indicating that the family tree had flourished luxuriantly before the author's grandfather, John Cline, moved south to Virginia, and became the owner of a farm in a locality which is now known as the city of Bristol. In Bristol he met and married an Englishwoman, Mary Hawk, and there his son, Jacob Leander Cline, the father of the author, was born. John Cline moved to Monroe County, Tennessee, in 1836. He died there of smallpox some time in 1864, during the period of the Civil War. His son, Jacob Leander Cline, father of Joseph Leander Cline, married Miss Mollie Wilson, whose father was George Wilson, a descendant of a Carolina and Georgia family. Her mother was Rebecca Harris, of Scotch-Irish descent, whose father had been a slave owner of Madisonville, Tennessee.

Jacob Leander Cline, father of the author of this volume, whose name often appears in the following pages, told his boys that his grandfather came to America with the early settlers in quest of just one of those four aims set forth in the Atlantic Charter—the goal of freedom of speech.

The struggle of those first settlers, after their traveling thousands of miles across the sea to achieve that one supreme ambition, must have been characteristic of the Cline blood. Jacob L. Cline, after the death by smallpox of his pioneering father John Cline, deeded to his sister, to her husband, Greggs Bledsoe, and to their children, his entire interest in their legacy, a small farm in Monroe County, Tennessee. Then, clothed only in a shirt and trousers, barefooted and penniless, he set forth to make his own way in the world. A hard, steady, thrifty worker, he rented a farm, of which he later became the owner. Before his death he had built up his property to the value of more than ten thousand dollars.

Jacob Leander Cline and wife Mollie Cline, father and mother of Joseph Leander Cline, lived the remainder of their life in Monroe County, Tennessee, where all of their children were born. There were ten children—six girls and four boys. They are listed herewith, with the exception of two girls, who died in infancy:

Isaac Monroe Cline, who married Cora May Ballew, of Missouri, when in charge of the Weather Bureau station at Abilene, Texas. His wife was drowned in the Galveston Hurricane. He is now the owner of "The Art House" in New Orleans, Louisiana.

Alice Cline, who married Jake Summit, of Monroe County, Tennessee. Both deceased.

Maggie Cline, who died at the age of three years.

George Cline, who married Juretta Mangus, of Monroe County, Tennessee. Both deceased.

Sallie Cline, who married Frank Airheart, of Monroe County, Tennessee. She deceased. He is living in Scottsboro, Alabama.

Cora Cline, who married Arthur Brakebill (now deceased), of Monroe County, Tennessee. She is now living on her farm near Knoxville, Tennessee.

Thomas A. Cline, who married Alice Cook (now deceased). He is now living on his farm near Claremore, Oklahoma, where he is a member of the Government Farm Board.

Joseph Leander Cline, author of this volume, who married Ula Jean Jackson, of Chambers County, Texas (now deceased). He became the father, and his wife the mother, of one son, Durward Jackson Cline, who married Katherine Gray, of Dallas, Texas, on September 30, 1925. They are the parents of two sons, Durward Jackson Cline, Jr., and Gerald Joseph Cline.

CHAPTER I

FAMILY AND EARLY LIFE

I was born on September 20, 1870, in Monroe County, Tennessee, on the farm of my father, Jacob Leander Cline, situated between Madisonville and Sweetwater. My early life was spent there, as one of a family of seven living children, four boys and three girls. It was there that I came to learn everything there was to know about farm life. On the dark, cold winter mornings, my brothers and I would start the day early by eating breakfast, feeding the livestock, and being off to the fields by daylight. We were kept hard at it until dark, plowing, chopping, and doing all the odd jobs connected with rural existence. Then, at night, there was the stock to feed again. Between times, there were planting, cultivating, harvesting, hiving bee swarms and robbing the hives of honey. Other duties were buying, feeding and selling beef cattle, selling grain, and repairing machinery. All these things I learned to do, and to do well.

Farming in those days was likely to develop qualities of ingenuity to a marked degree. I have often made shift to repair a broken plow-line by substituting a length of grapevine cut from nearby woods. I did this in order to save a trip back to the barn and thereby lose little time from my labors. When there was no metal lap-ring handy, I have peeled a section of hickory bark as a device for re-connecting a broken drawing chain. Once we had a coffee scarcity which had nothing to do with War Production Boards or Offices of Price Administration. I suggested what turned out to be a very successful blend of parched corn and peas ground together. I fashioned shingles, split rails, hewed logs "to the line" for construction of houses, and cut and threshed wheat, as well as oats and clover seed. In the horse-and-buggy days of 1884, I devised and built a kiln as a home dehydration plant for drying perishable fruit and vegetables. It had several trays and two fireplaces. I was proud of that kiln. I am still proud of it.

I tanned squirrel hides for shoe laces, which served their purpose of lacing the brogan type of footwear far better than did the laces to be had in the stores. At harvest time, I followed my father's thresher, stacking the straw. At this job I became very proficient, being the only one of us who could make the straw stacks turn sufficient water to preserve them through two winters. Straw was a big factor in feeding animals in East Tennessee in those days. I still cannot enjoy eating the present-day hominy and sauerkraut when I compare this food with the homemade tasties made on the farm. It may here be pointed out that we didn't have to buy vitamins or patronize bran "health centers" in those days, in order to stay well. In contrast with the farmers of today, we were able to produce everything we needed to eat except sugar, salt, coffee, tea and clothing. These commodities were purchased with money derived from sales on the local market. Some cash was generally left over, and this was placed in the bank for a rainy day. We never thought of complaining about the expenditure of a little additional effort. Even when I was attending college, I have often walked, on Saturdays, a distance of five miles to my father's home, there to swing a cradle all day in the wheat fields where the hired men were cutting. I often wonder how many boys away from home, in school or at college, would be capable of a like effort today.

Our land lay in a green valley, surrounded for a distance of several miles by the foothills of rugged mountain country, most of which lay to the southeast. The majority of the hill and mountain farmers owned one or two milch cows, which, in spring and summer, generally grazed over the unfenced natural growth overflowing the mountain ranges. As feed grew scarce in winter, the calves usually became a liability to their owners, and the owners in most cases, were then ready to sell. Most of the buyers of the calves rode on muleback up the mountain.

These junkets gave us our first real experience in business methods. Each winter, my father was accustomed to say, "boys, get ready for the calf-buying time right after Christmas." When the day came, my father would lead the way up the mountainside, with my brothers, George and Tom, and myself following. At one place, George would be the buyer. Tom would probably preside at the next meeting place. I would generally take charge of the bargaining. Father would remain an interested observer until the dickering was well under way. When we arrived at an amount which he considered to be the worth of that particular animal, he would tap us on the leg with a switch which he always carried with him. If our maximum offer ever failed to obtain our calf, I don't recall it. The names and figures of each particular transaction were then jotted down in the little memorandum books which we all carried. For each calf purchased, the owner would be paid a dollar down, with the stipulation that he would receive the balance when the animal was brought to Madisonville, the Monroe county seat. The time arranged for the final payment was four o'clock in the afternoon of January thirty-first. Thus the deal was closed without the need of any bill of sale or contract. These informal agreements took place every winter and not one dollar of the deposits was ever lost.

It was in this manner that, throughout our early life, my father instilled into his boys the art of commerce. The result was that all four of the "Cline boys," George, Isaac, Tom and I, were successful, and most of the property we acquired was obtained by wise trading. My father could put his little leg-tapping trick to work on bigger deals than calf buying.

Before my father bought the farm on which he was living, the place was offered by the owner for sale at auction. There was a road running from the flour mill on Bat Creek, through the middle of the farm, nearly a mile from the house, to Madisonville, the county seat. My father did not want to buy the farm until the road was changed so as to run past the house in which he lived.

Here, however, he ran head-on into the opposition of a wealthy and influential neighbor, owner of the above-mentioned flour mill. It was a fight between a thrifty and moderately well-to-do David and the Goliath of that locality. The fight went on for years before my father won his point with the county commissioners and the road was changed to suit his demands.

Mr. Johnston, otherwise Goliath, vowed vengeance. When the auction was announced, he evidently thought that his opportunity had arrived. He was heard to remark, "Jake Cline will pay for that road deal when he tries to buy the farm."

When the bidding began, my father mingled with the crowd, apparently only an onlooker. A poorly dressed man from the mountains, a stranger in that vicinity, was doing a lot of bidding. Many in the crowd audibly wondered if he had the money to make good his bids. Goliath (Mr. Johnston) was frankly puzzled. How could he bid against Jake Cline when the latter was not even interested? He was entirely ignorant of the fact that the roughly dressed mountaineer was bidding on my father's instructions; the fact was made clear when the auctioneer announced that the property was sold to the stranger and my father stepped forth to claim it as his own. The arrangement had been made long before the sale, and the trick, which was a novel one in that part of rural Tennessee, worked to perfection.

My father was a shrewd bargainer in a trade, and, as I have said, his example in this respect proved very valuable to his sons in later years. However, where no deal was involved, both he and my mother were the soul of generosity. We had four large orchards, two producing apples, one peaches, and the other plums. Wild strawberries, black-berries, and dewberries grew on the land in profusion. None of the fruit, except that which was processed in the home-built dry kiln previously mentioned, was ever sold. Neigh-bors and farmers, from twenty miles away and more, were privileged to come at will to our place and to gather and carry away apples and peaches by the cartload, both for eating fresh and for sun-drying.

Furthermore, there being no large town nearby, and, therefore, no bank within ten or twenty miles of us, my father always kept a little fund for loans to meet his neigh-bors' small emergency needs. This cash was handed out on request from the bureau drawer, and neither note nor in-terest was ever exacted. The sole record of these loans of a few dollars was a little notation specifying the date when the borrower agreed to repay the advance. The money was not always repaid on time, and, in many instances, the bor-rowers stated that they had been unable to sell corn, wheat, or oats. I have never once heard my father refuse to grant them the requested extension on the loan.

Indeed, the above cases were exceptions, for the people of that class paid their debts promptly in those days. My father was as precise on this point as any man I have ever known. To what extent he honored even the smallest obligation, I came to know on the day of his funeral. The presiding minister told the following story to illustrate some of my father's good qualities.

A friend of my father's, one Richard Hudson, who was himself present at the funeral service, told how he had looked out of his window one bitterly cold and stormy day and observed a solitary horseman, fighting his way through the wind and heavy snowdrifts to the Hudson house. At closer range, he recognized the rider as his friend Jacob Cline, who, upon entering the house, held out a penny to him.

Hudson was a buyer and seller of cattle. In one of his deals with my father, they had failed by one cent to arrive at the correct change. It was for that reason that my father rode ten miles through a blizzard to bring the correct change on the appointed day. I am proud to record here that it was said among his associates, that some of his good qualities had been passed on to his sons. He gave us all much good counsel. I recall one bit of half-serious, half-humorous advice:

"You'll soon be going out in the world where you will meet with many ups and downs. Never believe anything you hear and only half that you see. Then you may be right half the time. You'll be damned if you do and damned if you don't. Just do the best you can. Angels can do no more."

The first twenty years of my life were happily spent, working on my father's isolated farm in Monroe County, Tennessee. I went to school and, in my spare time, roamed the mountains, hills, valleys, and "knobs" of East Tennessee. I can see the green countryside now with the blue mists hanging from the tree-tops. I can still taste the wild blackberries and dewberries. There were chestnuts, hazelnuts, red and black haws, and chinquapins in profusion, plus hickory nuts, pawpaws, cherries and mulberries—the wild delicacies from the "spring-branch" bottoms. Best of all, there were the persimmons and the pies made from the fruit.

Every Sunday the family would attend services in the primitive little church. Afterwards, we would go foraging in the woods, and would sometimes find a fat opossum. Taken home and fed for a few days, the opossum always found its way into the pot. When properly prepared and cooked this animal makes as clean and appetizing a dish as pig's feet. We kept several gum trees notched for our chewing gum, and we also chewed the clean, woodsy red and slippery elm bark in the spring. As an experiment, we tried eating the wild Indian turnips and badly burned our mouths.

Boyhood's thrills, like boyhood's appetites, leave behind them the keenest and most lasting impressions. Our rough, half-wild country had its own quota of "hants," as the country people called them. My own most shivery experience in that line came one dark night, in the intense gloom of some woods which formed a background for many of our community's most prized ghost stories.

The people in that vicinity were unfamiliar with the ways of the back-country Negroes, who were rare in that part of the country. A group of the neighborhood boys, of which I was one, hiked five miles into the hills, to a point at which was located a Negro settlement. We intended to be eavesdroppers at a big camp meeting and to gratify our curiosity by hearing a Negro preacher.

When we were about a mile's distance from the scene, the Negroes' deep, mellow voices floated through the woods to our ears. As we drew nearer, we could hear, with increasing clarity, the words of the song. As I remember them, they were about as follows:

"Get right, members in de church,
    Lawdy!
For Sunday is the sacramental
    Day! Day!

Ole Satan wears a run-down shoe,
And if you don't min', he will slip it on you—
Get right, members in de church—
Lawdy!"

When we started on our homeward way, the night seemed
darker than usual. I made up my mind to take a short cut
through the fields, even though the way led past the
"Haunted Woods." The rest of the boys dropped off one
by one and went their separate roads. As I struck out alone
in the direction I had chosen, I felt myself growing less bold
every minute. All the stories I had ever heard about those
woods came swiftly back to me.

For example, there was that tale about Mr. Ransom
Moree, a neighbor of ours, who had become lost in the
woods one rainy night. It was said that he was lured off on
some mysterious trail by an eerie will-o'-the-wisp that
danced before his eyes the whole night long. The rumor got
around that he nearly died in consequence of this experience.

Then I remembered a tale that my uncle told about being
with a hunting party in that locality, when he suddenly became aware of a headless woman, wrapped in a misty veil,
floating up the hollow. My uncle himself informed me
that she gave the hunters a thin, quavering hail. She then
whispered, in a voice that resembled the soughing of wind
through the tree-tops, that she was looking for a jug of
whiskey that her husband had buried there some fifteen years
before. I stoutly denied the truth of this anecdote, but his
companions in the adventure backed him up and declared
that it was true.

When I drew near these woods, my courage nearly for-
sook me. The trees looked dreadfully large and held menac-
ing shadows. But it was either the woods or a walk of some

miles around by the main road. I summoned all my forti-
tude, took a long breath, and boldly plunged into the half-
mile strip of woodland ahead of me.

The dried leaves rattled beneath my feet. They had fallen
so thickly that the path was hidden. I was unable to follow
it, save by straining my eyes for the dim, narrow slit in
the trees above. Suddenly a huge black mass loomed just
ahead. A big tree had fallen down, blocking my way. Rather
than pick up my trail around it and perhaps not be able
to find the path again, I decided to climb over it.

I scrambled to the top of the trunk. Swish! Swish! Something shot through the quaking leaves. Something heavy,
that ran the entire length of the prone trunk. Suddenly the
sounds ceased. The Thing, whatever it was, had turned
around to face me. With a tumultuously beating heart, I
jerked out my pocketknife. Then I whistled, yelled, and
stamped on the tree, making a terrific noise. The noise which
I set up was followed by a dead silence. I concluded that
the Thing was waiting for me to make the first move, which
I did by jumping from the trunk. Instantly, I was seemingly caught by the feet and flung headlong forward. My hat
flew off in another direction. For an instant I lay still, trying
to control the overwhelming fear that possessed me. When I
struggled to my feet, I heard the same threshing sounding
in the branches of the tree and the bushes farther off. The
Thing was moving away from me. This time it ran for a
considerable distance; then turned, and seemed about to come
back. At this point it made its first sound—a long-drawn
"boo-o-o-o," followed by another. I gave a shaky laugh and
my knees grew firm again. Now I definitely knew what the
intruder was. I called out loudly, "You old fool sow! If I
had a gun, I would kill you." The beating of my heart became normal. Everything was clear. The sow's pigs had
made the first noise, running along the trunk. The litter

must have been at their meal in the path beneath the sheltering bole. The sow had upset me when I stepped upon her.
If she hadn't given vent to those grunts, I would never
have known what the whole thing was about. And in this
way, another juicy ghost story was lost to the ones already
told about that locality.

Incidentally, the hogs that strayed through the thick
wooded areas of East Tennessee often grew lean, wild, and
speedy as deer. An example of this occurred in a drove of
hogs which we allowed to rove in the wooded range that
stretched across our farm. In order to keep them domesti-
cated, we called them daily for a feeding of corn. One day
they didn't answer our call; and from that time on, they ran
wild over our grounds and in the high "sage" fields of an adjoining place. We sometimes caught a glimpse of them, but
we couldn't catch them. Their capture was ultimately brought
about by the construction of a large pen across a hole in the
fence, where the trampled grass indicated that the animals
had frequently passed from one farm to another. We
herded the unwary fugitives towards the woods, and they
ran through the hole into the trap. A door was sprung behind them and they were our prisoners. It was not easy to
take them from the pen, as they fought desperately. We
finally caught them, one by one, with a rope, a noose, and
a forked pole. After we had lassoed them, we had to fend
them off from us, or they would have torn us to pieces.

I remember another thrill that I had in those days—a
thrill not unmixed with a sense of deep pity. That was
when a "wild man" was captured in the nearby mountains.
For a long time the story had gone the rounds, among
sober, reliable people, that a wild creature resembling a man
had been seen running through the woods. One day it actually came to pass that officers brought him to town and penned
him up, much as we penned up the hogs on our farm.

Among the sightseers who came to view him were my father, my brothers, and I.

He certainly looked like a wild man. He was covered with hair from head to foot. His eyes showed no single gleam of intelligence and his behavior was that of an animal. His efforts at speech were like the jabber of an ape. As I look back on it now, it was a soul-sickening spectacle to see a human being, if one could call him that, in such a pitiable plight. To a half-grown lad, it was just an exciting episode.

Another unnatural product of Mother Nature was a flippered calf, one of the oddest animal freaks that I ever saw, which was born on the farm of my uncle, George Cline. This farm was located some miles from ours, in the same county. One day I had occasion to go to Madisonville on business, and met Uncle George downtown. There was an unusually large number of people on the streets, and I asked him the cause of the excitement.

"You won't believe it, Joe, when I tell you," he replied. "It's a calf with fins. I found it when I went into the field yesterday to attend a cow that had calved. The calf has a normal head and body, but it has no legs. There are fins where the legs should be. I would hardly believe it unless I saw it with my own eyes. It's in the room yonder. Go and take a look at it."

I went in. The calf was there, all right. It was lying down, but occasionally it hitched itself around with its fins, which it operated with a fish-like movement. The poor little beast lived and was later sold to an itinerant show. The owner, however, lost in the deal, as it was subsequently reported that the Humane Society had taken the calf away from him.

Our county had its crazy person, as almost every community has at one time or another. This one was a woman, of whom all the children were desperately afraid. The muddy, unpaved road to the public school, four miles from my home, ran directly in front of the house in which she lived. It was whispered that she was locked in a wired-up room, but was sometimes allowed liberty by her family to go out in the air and sunshine. One day I thoughtlessly stopped by her house to gather some haws. When I had finished and looked up I found that the crazy woman had crept up close to me and now stood in the road, barring my path. I suspect that I looked rather frightened. Here was something that might have made a good nightmare, and it was actually happening. I stared at her wholly unable to speak. Her gray hair was straggling over her shoulders and her black eyes glared at me. She asked me a question in a thin, high voice:

"Do you know that there is a tooth out of my comb?"

My own teeth were chattering so that I could scarcely answer. Finally I gasped out:

"No."

She crept a little closer to me.

"Well, what do you know, then?"

I knew only one thing, and that was that I wanted to get away from her and in double-quick time. As she turned her head a moment, I sprinted past her at lightning speed and caught up with my companions. Never again did I loiter in that vicinity.

Another time I survived the attack of a "screech owl," as they called the big bird in those parts. While I was passing through a wooded hollow, a blow on my head knocked my hat off. I picked it up and put it more firmly on my head. Another blow knocked it off again. Peering through the darkness around me, I could barely discern an owl, which was fluttering in a nearby tree. It came at me again, but I ducked and evaded it. Before it could make a fourth onslaught, I had taken myself swiftly out of range. It was an eerie experience, coming, as it did, out of the blackness of the night.

Perhaps our most thrilling devil's haunt was a harmless-looking pool on our farm called "Boyd's Pond," about an acre in size. It was the only swimming pool in the neighborhood, being too deep for non-swimmers, and large enough to offer a challenge to the venturesome.

A local swimmer one day made the boast that he would "swim the pond four times or go to Hell." After these words, he dived swiftly in and began his marathon, while his companions watched him in awe-stricken silence. He swam the distance three times, apparently without any trouble. Then, when he had nearly completed swimming the fourth and last lap—the tragedy happened. Swiftly his body began to whirl around—his hands flew up helplessly, and he was sucked underneath the water. He never came up to the surface. The diving for his body went on for days, but it was never found. Some people were of the opinion that God had given him what he asked for. More sensible minds arrived at the conclusion that the mud bottom of the little lake had suddenly caved in at the spot where he was swimming, and that he was dragged into a "sink-hole," after which the mud filled in above him.

I knew from my own experience how suddenly those cave-in's could occur around Boyd's Pond. I had been plowing one day in one of the three fields that touched the water's edge, forming a point at which the stock could drink. When I stopped work in the evening, I left the plow standing there. Next morning, when I returned, leading the horse, a large hole had formed on the spot and there was no sign of the plow anywhere. I listened above the hole and could hear water running. When I left home, many years later, the hole was still there. For my part, I paid no attention to the stories told about Boyd's Pond and did not fear it very much. Once I even made the swim three times, but had no desire to try it the fourth time.

It was strictly a swimming hole for men and was so far off the highway that nobody thought of swimming suits. One hot day, however, as we were getting ready to cool ourselves by a dip, we espied some obviously feminine clothing arranged in neat little piles on the bank. A dense pine thicket ran close to the water at that point. We suddenly realized that some startled damsels must have fled into the brush at the sound of our voices. We turned and left, giving up our swim in response to the mute appeal of those eloquent little heaps of filmy things.

The most gruesome event of my early years was the almost premature burial of a near neighbor and family friend. Some people by the name of Lowery lived on an adjoining farm. The grandfather of the household had reached an advanced age. For years he had been unable to walk, the upper part of his body being paralysed. After an unusually severe seizure, the doctor had pronounced him dead. As was customary in our community, the neighbors began to dig the grave. Some of the men labored at building the coffin, and the women assisted in preparing the shroud. I was at the cemetery, digging with the others. The grave was nearly completed when a rider on horseback raced up to the spot, shouting at the top of his lungs: "Stop! Stop!"

We all turned around with our mouths open.

"Mr. Lowery is not dead," he yelled. "He's alive."

Then he told us that, when the sorrowing relatives were laying the body in the coffin, the "corpse" was seen to move slightly. The breast rose and fell. The "dead" man was breathing. It seems that the act of changing the position that the old man had held so long, had renewed the life that must have been merely dormant when the burial preparations were under way.

And, indeed, he lived on for three days more. Then death really returned to claim him. He was buried in a coffin that had been completed before his death, and laid to rest in a grave that was partly dug before he died.

CHAPTER II

SCHOOL DAYS AND TEACHER

Twenty years, about one-fourth of the allotted span of human life, I passed on my father's farm, or in school. My school years, spent at the public school of the county, were much like those of any other youngster at that time.

One little triumph I achieved as a schoolboy was rather amusing, and gave indication of a quality, the power of observation, which stood me in good stead in my later scientific work, and contributed much toward my rating as one of the best United States Weather Observers.

On one night every week, there was a magnificent old-time spelling bee at the schoolhouse, with two team captains named to "choose up" the contestants. According to the custom, they drew for first choice. I was usually chosen by the winner, as I was reputed to be the school's foremost speller.

On the occasion in question, one word was passed up and down the opposing lines, as each contestant misspelled it and sat down. It came to me last, and I spelled it correctly. When it was made known that my spelling was correct, I was the hero of the evening. I was the boy who "knew the spelling book."

The word was "restaurant," and I hadn't got it out of a book. I had seen it on a sign outside an eating place in the town of Sweetwater, where I had gone with my father to make some purchases the same afternoon.

Another episode of my school days may serve to throw light on what an impetuous, downright little fellow I was. I was both fond and proud of my hunting dog. One day, when I was out with him hunting, a bigger boy in the neighborhood—one of those "born bullies"—happened along and began throwing rocks at the pup. I was filled with indignation. What was more, I was carrying a shotgun. I gave a yell to attract the youth's attention and, when he looked up, he was looking right down the barrel of my weapon.

"If you ever throw another rock at that dog, I'll shoot you," I told him. Judging by his frightened expression, I must have looked as though I meant it. At any rate, the rock throwing ceased.

Despite that initial victory, it turned out that I hadn't finished with that boy. On a later occasion, the people of the community were assembling for one of the periodical evening meetings in the Union Hill Schoolhouse. I had arrived early. So had the same bully, with some bigger boys. We were all waiting on the stage, at the back of the room, for the evening's program to begin.

My neighborhood enemy began to amuse himself by annoying two orphaned lads, both smaller than himself. I intervened, warning him to keep his hands off them or look to me for trouble. Still nursing some bad blood from our previous encounter, the boy said, "You're a liar."

Again I saw red. I struck him in the face, as he stood on the edge of the stage, knocking him down into the first row of benches. I remained on guard waiting for a counterattack, but some of the bigger boys took charge of us and suppressed what had all the earmarks of a budding battle of the century.

The foregoing are merely a few of the impressions retained of those earlier days. I applied myself to my books and, after duly completing the lower school course, entered Hiwassee College, which was located near Madisonville, about five miles from my home. This college stood by a small stream which bore the picturesque name of Bat Creek. Instead of taking quarters in the main college building, I rented one of the single-room dormitories, which had been built for students of lesser means. Each of these rooms was heated by an open fireplace and divided into a "study" in one corner, a "dining room" in another, and the "bedroom" in yet another. In that room I slept, studied, and cooked my own meals. Thrift and hard work were, by now, second nature to me. I brought my own firewood from the farm, five miles away. The water I used for household purposes was transported from a large cool spring nearly a mile from my living quarters.

My monthly bill for food averaged four dollars and eighty cents. I purchased eggs from nearby farms at about eight to twelve cents a dozen. Fresh country butter could be purchased at from ten to fifteen cents a pound, corn-fed pork and cured hams for four and one-half cents a pound. Fresh vegetables could be had at corresponding prices. Some of these vegetables I sold to the residents of other dormitories. I lived well. A rich student from Chattanooga, who once dined with me, said it was better food than he and other students were regularly eating at the college mess hall, where they paid the munificent sum of ten dollars a month. Those where happy, wholesome times to look back upon, even now, when the atmosphere and conditions which made them possible have gone forever.

To pay the costs of my tuition, I made a contract with the superintendent of the institution to fence in the campus at ten cents per hour. By working after four o'clock every afternoon, while the other boys were playing baseball, I earned enough to pay my tuition. It may be well to remark here that baseball was the leading sport of those times, football being then unknown.

One of my spare-time and classroom hobbies was public speaking. I greatly enjoyed debating activities and was considered by the school to be unusually good at both of them.

I was elected president of the Aerolethean Society, one of the institution's two debating organizations. We had no Greek letter fraternities, and these groupings partially fulfilled the purpose subserved by societies in the modern college, besides satisfying the natural desire of youth to argue a point.

Just before Christmas each year the graduating classes held a public debate, which was a big event with the citizens of the locality. Each of the two societies named a declaimer as a champion at these public contests. I was elected to represent the Aeroletheans, and another student, named Willbanks, who had specialized in elocution, was chosen by the Aermothesians. In addition to this, each side had its two debaters.

In matching the training of Willbanks, I had the advantage of practical experience in speaking from the time I was a small boy. Almost since I could talk I had taken part in public entertainments, including Christmas tree and like celebrations, at public schools and in churches in our settlement.

As in the case of the boy bully, I seemed to be continually crossing swords—but this time intellectually—with Willbanks. Each Wednesday, all students were required to assemble in the main hall, where selected orators were designated to recite a bit of poetry or to make a short speech. Other students would be named by the faculty to criticise any mistakes made by the speaker.

Willbanks spoke first, but faltered at several crucial points, having failed to memorize his address. Once his hesitation was so pronounced that he had to be prompted by an aid from the audience, who held a copy of his address.

When my turn came, I recited "I Dreamt That I Dwelt in Marble Halls" so correctly that I was declared the winner. The Madisonville newspaper, in recounting the event, stated: "At the Annual Public Debate, yesterday evening, Joseph Cline's speech was voted the best on the program. He was the recipient of numerous flowers from the young ladies present, as the outstanding orator of the occasion."

At another time, Willbanks, who was a law student, was one of the speakers. Being selected as one of the critics, I arose when I heard what I believed to be a slip, and said: "I differ with Mr. Willbanks."

Before I could state my objection, however, Willbanks parried the coming criticism by retorting: "I wish to correct Mr. Cline. He should have said, 'I differ from,' not 'I differ with.'"

That was a puzzler. The audience, and even the faculty, took sides. At the end of the period, no valid decision was reached and the disputed point was finally passed over to the following Wednesday. At the latter date, however, I walked off with the honors. The faculty secretary announced that after considerable difficulty in deciding between the opposing viewpoints, the faculty had agreed that "In opinions, people differ *with* each other," while "stars differ *from* each other in appearance."

Thus, from the beginning, I was imbued with the spirit of the orator, and I always enjoyed these exercises and the small triumphs I achieved from them. I made my initial distinction in college when I was first assigned to take the floor. The president commented favorably upon the moral theme of the poem I selected, which he said the other students would do well to emulate. That I made the most of this inaugural good impression may be attested by the fact that I was among the very few of the institution's students, who were able to complete the full course without a single demerit.

On the practical side, also, I achieved something of a reputation. I possessed the knack of usually being able to hit upon the solution of a problem or the best way to handle a situation. This led to my acquiring somewhat of a name for infallibility.

For example, I had never enjoyed any acquaintance with gasoline engines. One day, while en route home, I was hailed by a group of farmers clustered about a motor-power grist mill that had ceased to run. They appealed to me for help. Nobody could start it, they said, and then stood aside with sighs of relief to "watch Joe get it going." It would have been no use to tell them that, although I had studied physics and the principles governing the operation of machinery, I had never tinkered with one of those things. They would just have smiled confidently and waved me on to the job.

There was nothing to do but go ahead and tackle the problem. I looked the mill over, tested the fuel and found the latter adequate. I then went over the connections and found one loose. I tightened it. Then I motioned to the operator of the machine to see if it would start now. He did, and it did. Then there were remarks: "Joe has done it again," and "You don't know how glad we were to see you coming." An enviable reputation, no doubt, but one that takes a good deal of living up to.

I was going to need all my capabilities. I was about to graduate. I had my own way to make in the world, at the age of twenty, one-fourth of my life rather successfully behind me—as I fancied. I subsequently progressed to the degree of Bachelor of Science, in the class of May 14, 1891.

I applied for a position as teacher in a public school, and obtained one at Mount Vernon, Tennessee. The pay was twenty-five dollars a month. Armed with my state teaching certificate, which I had obtained from the State Normal School at Madisonville, Tennessee, by passing the required examination that summer, I arrived, on a Saturday in the fall of 1891, upon the scene of what were to be my pedagogic labors, beginning the following Monday.

In that farming community, even the members of the school board and many of the prospective students were in the fields, threshing wheat. Feeling comfortably at home in this familiar farm setting, I introduced myself and chatted for a while with the residents. I arranged for board at the home of Dr. McCullough, contracting to pay five dollars a month, with the proviso that I walk with the youngsters of the household to school each morning. The walking was easy, as the distance was only a mile, and my active life had made such exercise less an inconvenience than a pleasure. My room was a large one, with the usual furniture and a luxurious feather bed. Laundering, ironing, and other necessities were furnished without additional charge. This enabled me to save about twenty dollars a month out of the small pay I received there.

On the first evening I spent in my new home I began to hear rumors of future discord. Some of the boys I had met in the field that afternoon had been trouble-making students during the preceding school year. For two years, these and other larger boys had led my predecessor a rather strenuous life. I was informed that they had intimidated him with cursing and rowdyism, and had openly promised to "run the school and that young boy we've got for a new teacher, just the way we always did." I made a mental note of that.

So, before entering the schoolroom for my first appearance before the student body, I wrote out a set of rather drastic rules. In Tennessee schools, at that time, the teacher retained supervision over pupils for the entire period between their leaving home and returning again in the afternoon. One of the rules therefore, forbade any students to climb over farm fences into fruit orchards, on penalty of receiving a whipping, or worse, of being expelled. Another provision of the code required all students to be at their desks within five minutes after the bell rang.

Armed with these resolutions, I fared forth to school on Monday morning with my charge, the young McCullough boy. Nearing the building, I noticed a group of the bigger boys—actually, they were man-sized, and, by their appearance man-eaters also—standing together near the entrance. I learned afterwards, from the head of the school board, that they were then in the act of completing an agreement to work together against my efforts to control them, and to "show that they were going to run the school."

Seeming not to notice their rather belligerent attitudes, I walked past them and went inside. I called the school to order, and as an opening exercise read a chapter from the New Testament. Then I read the rules that I had made out, and emphasized the fact that I meant to have them obeyed. I next asked if all present had their grade-rating cards, as required by state law. I learned that many of them did not. The outgoing teacher had not seen to it, although the law had been in effect for two years.

I had, therefore, to devise some method of impromptu grading. I decided, accordingly, to let their spelling ability decide their respective ratings. I called them all to the front of the room and lined them up according to size. I then explained that they would be given words to spell, for tentative grading, which would be subject to later revision as I became familiar with their various capacities.

Immediately the trouble commenced, as I had expected. One of the older scholars of about my own size started the game planned for the new teacher, by spelling the word given him, but failing to pronounce it properly. I corrected him, and again he rather elaborately mispronounced the same word. I kept on giving him words and the same thing kept happening. Finally I reached into my pocket, drew out my pocketknife, and opened it.

I said to another student, "Take this knife and cut me a good switch. Be sure it is a good switch, or I will get one myself and use it on you. I don't like to whip anybody, but when I do, I whip hard enough to make sure that I will be obeyed in the future."

Another big fellow rose, as if in response to a signal of some kind.

"You won't whip him, Professor," he shouted. "He is my brother. The boy stutters."

Instantly I had the new rebel by the shoulder. I gave him a good shaking.

"I am running this school, not you," I told him. "If you ever again interfere with my correction of a pupil, you will get the harder whipping of the two. Do you understand me?"

The boy said, "Yes, sir."

Then I turned back to the first source of the trouble, and gave him several new words to spell and pronounce—and, this time, he did so correctly. The hickory switch, duly brought in and handed to me, was hung in a conspicuous place—and the crisis was over. There never was another. The president of the board, long afterwards, told me that his daughter, who was in the schoolroom at the time, had described the whole affair at the supper table that night. He added that, after hearing the story, he had remarked to his wife, "Cline is going to run that school."

I did run it. It is only fair to state at this point that the youth who had touched off the fireworks by refusing to pronounce the words correctly, did stutter when spelling words containing certain vowels. When he later became obedient, I promptly commended him. However, I had taken my stand, and settled the dormant rebellion before it got well under way.

The story of my modest, but, to me, important victory traveled abroad like wildfire. Word was passed far and wide that the scholars had been disciplined at last. One incident was typical of the favorable effect created. An elderly man brought his two sons, one twenty-one and the other twenty-four years old. He told me that he wanted to enter them in my school, at special tuition rates since he lived in another district.

"My oldest son was at Hiwassee College with you, Mr. Cline," he said. "He says that you can give him as much instruction as he could obtain there, and he can live at home. The younger boy has never studied, and I feel that you can make him work. Will you take them?"

"I'll gladly take them without any extra pay, if you will get the approval of the school board," I told the father, a powerfully built man of the mountaineer type. "But if I do, they must obey the rules just as these younger boys and girls do. If they don't, I shall send them home."

"If you send them home, Mr. Cline," said the gratified parent, with a stern look at his oversized sons, "I will promise them a harder whipping than you would give them."

He easily obtained the board's consent and was back with the boys next day. It was not long before both of them disobeyed the rules. Three days later, the older boy strayed away during a five-minute rest period and failed to return within the time allowed. The other pupils were openly curious as to the result of his refusal to obey authority. I drew forth my watch elaborately and publicly announced the time.

During recess I called his name. I told him that he was to remain at his desk and study until the afternoon session opened. I stated that he had violated one of the rules, which applied to all alike. Meekly he obeyed me.

The other brother waited a couple of weeks before he infringed on my regulations. He did so by stopping on the way home to climb the fence of an apple orchard. There had been many complaints made in the past about schoolboys purloining fruit from this same orchard. I learned indirectly that, in answer to the warnings of the other pupils, he said he "just wanted to get a few apples to eat."

At the close of school, I instructed him to stay until the others had departed. I told him plainly what I wanted to discuss with him. He waited. So did a large part of the student body, the latter remaining to giggle and peep through the windows. I suppose it was a queer sight. The schoolmaster younger than the pupil he was about to take (figuratively speaking) by the ear. Although I was aware that it was an unusual situation, I sent the audience home with the stern warning that they must obey still another rule —meaning the one that required them to go to their homes directly after school, or be punished themselves. Then I turned to the bigger and older boy in front of me.

I talked to him a little while, explaining the reason for the rule which he had violated. Then I asked him whether he wished to accept a whipping at my hands, or go home to stay. He replied without hesitation:

"I'll take a whipping from you, Mr. Cline. My dad meant it when he said that, if I should be sent home, he would give me a harder licking than you would give me."

"I'm sorry to whip a big boy like you," I answered. "However, to show me that you are really willing to take the punishment, you must take off your coat."

Off came his coat. When the switch came down—very lightly—he did not show resentment. He became one of my best pupils. Later, at the end of the school term, I missed him from among the pupils who attended the closing exercises. I went outside to look for him. Finally I came upon him, sitting on the bank of the spring branch that ran some little distance below the schoolhouse. He was crying.

I ran to him and asked him what was the matter. He answered in a shaken voice. "It is because school is over. It's the first school in which I have ever learned anything."

I put my arm, in a comforting way, around his shoulder. In this manner we walked down the green, shady path that led to the little frame schoolhouse—two very young men, teacher and pupil, together.

Some thirty years later, I received a letter bearing the postmark of a northwest Texas town. The signature was that of my former pupil. He asked if I was the Joseph Cline who had once taught a little school in Tennessee. I replied by asking him to visit my wife and me. He did not come, but it would have been a real pleasure to see him again.

I felt that my teaching venture was a success. Public attention from all points of the state was focused upon my tenure there. Sidney G. Gilbreath, state superintendent and a fellow graduate with me at Hiwassee, paid my school a visit during an inspection trip. He told me that wherever he went he heard good news of the school. He also voiced the wish that all his teachers were doing the same good work. To the board president he remarked that, judging from my accomplishments in school work, I would be heard from in later years.

Perhaps, to some extent, his prophecy was to be fulfilled. My name is to be found in the 1939-1940 edition of the *International Blue Book*, with my biographical data in three different languages—an honor bestowed only upon those considered worthy to be considered among the nation's notable figures. At the time of my retirement from the Weather Bureau, the Dallas *News*, in an editorial published October 2, 1940, made the following comment:

"Neighbors and friends of Dr. Joseph L. Cline will continue to ask and respect his opinion of next day's weather, even though he has put aside his meteorological instruments and quit reading the weather reports sent by distant stations. As head of the Dallas Weather Bureau since its establishment in 1913, Dr. Cline has made the city's residents so dependent on his forecasts that it may be a bit difficult for some to accept a new meteorologist.

"Dr. Cline's retirement at seventy years of age brings officially to a close one of the longest and most fruitful careers in the Weather Bureau. His reports on the 1900 Galveston Hurricane brought him favorable attention and a promotion to Porto Rico. Back in Texas, he was instrumental in establishing forest conservation work, training aviators in meteorology and prompting the growing of fruits and vegetables in the lower valley of the Rio Grande.

"Honored by many academic and scientific bodies, Dr. Cline has kept himself within easy reach of the many who wanted to know if rain would spoil their picnics, or if frost would kill their fall flowers, if left uncovered. Dallas people have liked Dr. Cline's variety of weather, and hope that his successor will bring as many pleasant days and evenings. As for 'Doc' himself, thousands of Dallas friends wish him happiness in the years of retirement to which he now looks ahead."

While I was weather observer in Galveston, Texas, I was once asked by the mayor and city aldermen to accept appointment as police commissioner. Again, while serving in my Weather Bureau post at Corpus Christi, Texas, I was requested by a committee, representing most of the city's outstanding businessmen, to run without opposition for the office of mayor. Both of these tendered honors I declined; preferring my work with the Bureau.

In addition to many other shorter articles on meteorological subjects, there follows a list of major lectures and articles written by me and published after my appointment to the Bureau:

"Crop Production in Texas, Compared With Temperature and Precipitation Departures, For Eight Years." Special Bulletin No. 2, Texas Weather Service.

"Normal Temperatures and Precipitation in Texas, for All Stations With Records Covering Five or More Years." Special Bulletin No. 5, Texas Weather Service.

"Climate of Texas in its Relation to the Cultivation of the Olive." Special Bulletin No. 6, Texas Weather Service. It was also published in *Gulf Coast Magazine* several years after its first appearance.

"Climate of Texas in its Relation to the Cultivation of the Apple." Published in the Galveston *News* and reprinted in pamphlet form.

"The Use of Frost and Temperature Warnings in Protecting Fruit and Truck-gardens." Published in the Galveston *News* and in the *Farmers Bulletin*, U. S. Department of Agriculture, in 1894.

"The Climate of Southwest Texas." *Gulf Coast Magazine*, Vol. 21, 1907, No. 3. When the issue was exhausted, this article was reproduced in another issue of the magazine.

"Frost Protection by Irrigation in Southern Texas." U. S. *Monthly Weather Review*, October 1914, page 591. Also, Weather Bureau Bulletin No. 542.

"Special Article on Puerto-Rico." *Monthly Weather Review*, 1902.

"Factors Affecting the Climate of Dallas County, Texas, and the Drouth of 1929." Dallas *Morning News*, November 18, 1929. Also reprinted.

"Climate-Agriculture." Published in newspapers and also in pamphlet form. A well-known statistician, who worked at the Dallas Cotton Exchange, stated that this was the best article written on agriculture up to that time. A cotton ginner who owned gins in many Texas counties expressed the desire that photostat copies be made and one be placed in the hands of every farmer in the counties in which he owned gins. A letter was therefore written to the Secretary of Agriculture in regard to the making and distribution of such copies.

CHAPTER III

EARLY DAYS IN TEXAS

Teaching school in that lovely Tennessee community was my first position. It was therefore with regret that I left it at the close of the term. Another place was offered me by wire, in Galveston, Texas, at a monthly salary of sixty dollars, as salesman—or "drummer," as it was called in those times—for a large printing concern just starting in business.

After I left for my work, a gratifying echo reached me from my teaching career. My father wrote me that he had met the president of the school board, who inquired where I had gone. When told that I had left for Texas, he asked my father to write me to return, as they wanted me back as teacher the following fall. He added that the job would be an all-year one, paid by money raised by public subscriptions added to the state funds. But I had already embarked upon what I found to be a, new and fascinating course of life.

Immediately I found that I had a battle of salesmanship upon my hands. Another large concern, long established in the territory, gave out that they had all the available business and neither used nor needed any solicitors. It was not long, however, before they altered their opinion, and put two salesmen in the field against me. I brought about this change of mind on their part, in spite of the fact that I never drank in a day when it was traditional that a drummer must drink with his customers in order to get business. I lost only one order because of my abstinence, and in doing so, I both taught and learned a lesson.

It was customary for every business house to maintain a beer or whiskey bar in the back rooms of the store. On the occasion to which I refer, a robust German merchant on whom I was calling invited me to a table in his bar. We sat down together and he listed a profitable order, after which he invited me to have a drink.

I said: "I never drink."

He looked surprised and not altogether pleased. I decided to give him a reason for declining that would appeal to his business sense.

"If I accepted your offer," I said, "it would only be right for me to ask you to have a drink. If I treated you, I would have to pay for it out of my own pocket or charge it to my company. To meet the increased expense, the company would be forced to raise prices on you and other customers. Therefore, in the end, you would have to pay for your drinks and mine too. Would you not?"

He said that he had never thought of it in that light. When I left, the unsigned order was still on the table.

But there was a final act to this little drama. The next time I passed that way I noticed the merchant sitting outside, at the rear of his store. I crossed the street, gave him a friendly handshake and went on my way, making no reference to business.

The next time I chanced to pass the merchant's store on the opposite side of the street, he called to me.

"Stop by next week," he shouted, "and I will give you an order."

I made the call at the suggested time and we repaired to the same table as before.

He began the conversation: "Young man, do you know you opened my eyes the last time we sat here?"

"How was that?" I innocently inquired.

"It was about the raise of prices to customers and who would end by paying for the drinks," he informed me.

I was not slow to comprehend his meaning. "You must have checked our prices and found them to be lower."

"I did," he replied. "Here is the order. It is a good one."

It was. From my little unrehearsed play the man learned a lesson. As for my lesson—perhaps the incident sharpened my selling ingenuity somewhat. My faith was strengthened in my ability to get along with my customers without the need of "social" drinking. After I had declined a glass of beer at the Garten-Verein, a big social drinking center, the fact that I was a non-drinker got around Galveston. It was said of me that I was the only man in the city who did not drink. It was perhaps because of this abstention that I was able to save some of my pay, although, on account of the higher cost of living, I saved less on sixty dollars in Galveston than I had on twenty-five dollars in Tennessee.

In spite of the fact that I had been successful as a salesman, I moved on to another job. I accepted an offer to work in the Gulf Colorado Railroad machine shops. The latter were largely unionized, but I was never asked to join a union. This may have been due to the fact that, only a few months later, I was to enter into what became my life work. One incident in the shops, however, remains indelibly imprinted upon my memory.

One day, in the latter part of the week, the foreman asked me if I would come down to the plant on the following Sunday. I asked him if any of the other men would be there. "I'll be there myself," he answered. I agreed to come.

When the two of us met at the shop that Sunday, the foreman led the way to a locomotive that required some final construction work to be done on it before it made its run on the following morning. After a morning's hard work, the finishing touches were put on the job by noon. The locomotive was now ready to make its run across Texas. It made the run without a single delay or mishap. I wondered why a twenty-one-year-old man had been chosen for this task. I learned later that not one locomotive recently turned out of that shop had made the full cross-state trip without a breakdown. The employees, it seemed, had banded together against the foreman, hoping to get the latter discharged. He had put his trust in me to do the job effectively. I did not fail him.

This happened in February, 1892. I continued to work for the railroad until March 22, 1892. I left it to accept an appointment as assistant observer for the Weather Bureau, under my brother, Dr. Isaac M. Cline, who was then section director for Texas, his assignment being in Galveston. I knew that Fred Fickett, my predecessor and a warm friend of both my brother and me, had accompanied General Greeley on his North Pole expedition. Mr. Fickett had done a fine piece of work with the Bureau. I determined to live up to this record and even better it, if I could.

I applied myself to my new job with all the diligence at my command. I studied night and day, absorbing all the current textbook material on meteorology, including "Abercromby." In addition to this, I made practice forecasts. In the meantime, I had done college graduate work and passed examinations successfully for the degree of Master of Arts and Doctor of Philosophy at Add-Ran University, Waco, Texas. With these degrees to my credit, I felt that I was equipped for any assignment.

All state forecasts at that time were issued at Washington, D. C., and telegraphed to each state section center. In Texas, they were telegraphed to Galveston for use in compiling local and state forecasts. The latter were then distributed to the public. The Government had not long before transferred the Weather Bureau from the United States Signal Corps to the jurisdiction of the Department of Agriculture, and Major Dunwoody, signal officer, who was con-

sidered the best weather forecaster of the time, was moved
to the Bureau.

On one occasion I had been left in charge of the station,
and a cold wave was sweeping in from Western Canada. Mr.
Dunwoody forecasted the cold wave would spread throughout Texas, and I relayed the news over the state. Next day,
however, the weather map made this forecast appear doubt-
ful, and Dunwoody changed his prediction to read: "Stationary temperature for most of Texas." I had read the map
differently, however, and telegraphed a warning requiring
the hoisting of a "colder weather flag at Dallas and all other
stations displaying weather flags."

Weather reports for the next day bore out my forecast.
They showed that the norther swept all the way across
Texas to the Gulf Coast. Had I proved to be wrong, I
should have risked a reprimand for altering the forecast of
my superior officer.

During the year 1894, when I had been in the Weather
Bureau two years, the President of the United States proclaimed an examination open to any citizen of the United
States, the winner to be elected to the office of Chief of the
Weather Bureau. The first step in the examination was to
be the writing of a thesis on the subject: "Weather Forecasts And How to Improve Them," to be signed by a nom de
plume, so that the three examiners would not be swayed
by the identities of the respective authors. The real names
went into sealed envelopes and were sent on to Washington
for checking against the pen names on the completion of the
tests.

Candidates with the ten highest grades were to report to
the National Capital for an examination in meteorology, in
addition to two weeks of competitive forecasting, using, in
the latter, only weather maps with dates and identifying
marks removed.

As I was new at this work, I hesitated for a long time to enter the contest. However, as it is not in my nature to shrink from a test, I duly wrote and mailed my thesis. Although I was not one of the group called to Washington, I learned afterwards that, had eleven candidates been chosen instead of ten, I should have been the eleventh. If I had been chosen, my life would have been different, and, perhaps, not so eventful in many ways. As it turned out, two contestants tied for first place, and then entered a run-off contest of actual forecasting.

At Galveston, I was making the most accurate observations in the Weather Bureau, heading, for each six-month period except one, the semiannual listing issued at Washington on a basis of accuracy by each observer in charge of the records. During that single less successful period, an observer named Ashenberger and I had only one error charged against each. My listing in the second place was due to my name coming farther down in the alphabetical order. Even then, one error in half a year is not a bad performance in any field of work.

My record was beginning to achieve recognition. Late in 1894 or early in 1895, I was asked to deliver a lecture before the Texas Horticultural Society at Bowie, as special representative of the railroad by which I had been previously employed. I prepared an article entitled "Climate of Texas In Its Relation to the Cultivation of the Olive." All articles by employees of the service had to be submitted to the Chief of the Bureau for his approval before their release, a rule which is still in force. Accordingly, I sent a copy to Professor Moore, the appointed Chief. It was quickly returned, accompanied by the requested authority to read and publish it, and in addition the following comment from Moore: "The article herewith returned is an excellent one and reflects great credit upon the author." At the foot of the typewritten page, and written in his own hand, was the more practical notation: "I have this day recommended the author for promotion." However, as it so happened that I had recently enjoyed a pay increase from nine hundred to one thousand dollars, the Chief's recommendation was disapproved by the Assistant Secretary of Agriculture. The Chief wired me to send a copy of my article to the Assistant Secretary in question. I complied, and also enclosed Special Bulletin No. 2, (Texas Weather Service) entitled: "Normal Temperature and Precipitation in Texas for All Stations With Records Covering Five or More Years."

This procedure had its effect. At Bowie, Texas, where I went to read the paper, I received a wire stating that the promotion had been allowed. After I had delivered the address, the president of the Society complimented me with the remark that it was "to my knowledge, one of the best and most instructive lectures ever presented before this Society."

The Weather Bureau was then in its infancy, and stood in need of stimulating material which might educate the public to the many beneficial phases of its services. Perhaps I possessed some of the qualities of vision necessary to obtain this result. I know that I was among the first lecturers and writers to advocate the cultivation of winter vegetables and semitropical fruits on the Texas coast. This was at a time when all the state was in cattle—when longhorns roamed the ranges, and southwest areas were literally crowded with these animals. Some time earlier, I had delivered a talk before the Society on the subject of "Protection of Crops From Frost and Freezing Temperatures," at another annual session which took place at the Texas Agricultural and Mechanical College, at College Station, Texas. I followed this up with an article dealing with "The Climate of the

Eastern Portion of the Coast District of Texas in Its Relation to the Cultivation of Fruit and Vegetables."

Because few or no vegetables or semitropical fruits were then being grown in Southern Texas, the newspaper published only excerpts from this paper, completely overlooking the following prophecy:

"The time will come when the East Texas Coast will be devoted principally to the cultivation and raising of winter vegetables and semitropical fruits."

I am rather proud of that glimpse into what actually became the future of this now famous area. My prophecy did not altogether go without recognition. The editor of the *American Meteorological Journal,* published in far-away Boston, wrote me that he had become interested in the newspaper comments on this lecture, and asked for the complete copy. The paper was subsequently printed in full in the issue of August, 1893, Vol. X, No. 4. About thirty-five years after its publication, Dr. Edwin J. Foscue, of the faculty of the Southern Methodist University, Dallas, called to ask me if I was the author of this old paper. When I told him that I was, he said:

"You should be proud to be the writer of that article. You have lived to see your prophecy come true."

While I was stationed in Galveston, the Spanish-American War occurred. The "Teddy Roosevelt Rough Riders," who made such a spectacular record at San Juan Hill, were organized in Texas. Most of the officers were visitors at the Weather Bureau from time to time, and seemed to take a keen interest in my work. They insisted that I should accept a commission in that famous outfit. I was sorely tempted to go with them and wired the Chief of the Weather Bureau for authority to do so. He replied by telegram that I was needed more at my Weather Bureau post in war time than in the army. I had, therefore, regretfully to abandon the idea.

A cold wave of unusual intensity crossed Texas in February, 1899. At Brownsville, the minimum reading was reported at twelve degrees, and at Galveston, the lowest mark was seven and one-half degrees. I took a reading that morning and telegraphed that shore ice had formed on Galveston Bay, something virtually unknown to Galveston residents.

Many large species of fish, particularly trout and redfish, feed in the bayous and shallow inlets extending from Galveston Bay in the direction of Houston, some sixty miles northward. The norther smashed head-on into an area of warm weather, taking effect so rapidly that fish as they were feeding became so chilled they were unable to reach deep water. Thousands of them, of all sizes, drifted in an icy state of torpor on the surface of Galveston Bay. They were actually too dulled to make their way beneath the surface of the water. Galvestonians and other Bay residents rowed out in boats, dipped out the live but torpid fish in nets, and returned to shore with their crafts loaded. Many a barrel of trout and red fish, both delicious when cleaned and cooked, were shipped from there to inland markets. Some were sent as far as Dallas, Texas, more than three hundred miles away, before the practice was halted by law enforcement officers.

An abnormally low tide resulted from the high north winds accompanying the cold wave. Wild ducks and geese had flown south in great numbers to the Texas coast. After the cold wave had disappeared, I went for a hunt along the shore of the Bay.

I caught sight of a flock of wild geese flying over in the vicinity of the mainland drawbridge leading to Virginia Point. I fired at them, knocking a couple out of the air into the water. Although crippled, they were able to swim, and they did, rapidly crossing the Bay towards the mainland. I followed, wading and shooting. I could hear the shot beating a tattoo against their wings, but they kept on swimming and I kept on wading in an odd aquatic marathon. The water was too deep to allow me to cut down much of the distance between myself and the birds. At the same time, because of the wind-affected tides, it was so shallow that I was actually able to ford the channel below the drawbridge, at a point where ocean-going vessels were normally able to cross.

Meanwhile, the geese had turned left at a point near the mainland, and were heading along the coast toward Brownsville, Texas. Although I was pretty well spent, I pushed on through the water across the Bay to the mainland. The geese won the race, but I had accomplished the unheard-of feat of wading clear across Galveston Bay. I was something of a nine-days' wonder to other residents of the countryside, who could hardly credit the truth of the story. The bridge itself was later washed away in the famous Galveston Hurricane of September 8, 1900. It has been replaced by another immediately above the spot where the original span stood— but the hurricane is another story, which will be told in a later chapter.

To conclude recounting the oddities resulting from the norther about which I am now writing, my nostrils were smitten by an almost overpowering stench as I approached the shore below Virginia Point. It was all but unbearable, and it did not require too much time to discern from whence it came. The source of the Gargantuan smell was fish—not a few scattered dead ones, but a nauseous fringe of them along the entire shore, four feet wide and one to four inches in depth, as they lined the shore. The fringe extended as far as eye could see. It was the chilled fish again, washed up on the sand when the tide went down.

Some years later, in Corpus Christi, Mr. Eli Merriman, editor of the Corpus Christi *Caller*, told me that the same condition prevailed along the Corpus Christi Bay and down towards Brownsville. He said his city had been forced to haul the dead fish off, because people living near the coast had been physically unable to endure the stench.

Legend, which is rich on and around Galveston Island, with its tales of Jean La Fitte, the buccaneer, and other local wonders, has it that even more severe cold smote the Texas Coast years before that. On that occasion, the old-timers relate, a man walked across the Bay on ice. It should be added that these narrators were politely hooted by their audience.

Galveston northers always seem to be uncovering something novel. My brother Isaac and I were ardent hunters as well as fishermen. We were out with our guns one day after a biting cold wave whose winds had blown much of the water out of the Bay, leaving small shallow lagoons in the land along the sea wall. We had walked out on the jetties intending to shoot flying ducks on the windward side, and to allow the wind to act as retriever by drifting them within reach.

We had not gone far when I saw a movement in the shallow water. It was made by what looked like a marine giant. "Ike," I exclaimed, in awe, "look at that fish! How about my taking a shot at it?"

My brother had another idea. He suggested that the fish was trapped away from deep water by sandbars along the shore, and that I wade out and get it. This would be a simpler and surer method of achieving success, he argued.

I removed my shoes, waded into the water, and made an effort to grasp the fish by its gills. I missed. The water was deep enough for the fish to be able to swim, although he could not submerge the fins along his back. He made a dash between my legs, drenching me with water from head to foot. I arose to my feet and tried a second time. This time my hold was secure, and I lugged it to shore—a twelve-pound redfish. When I staggered through the Galveston streets with that enormous fish on my shoulder, goggle-eyed crowds lined the sidewalks.

"Where'd you catch that whale, Joe?" was the universal query. Their mystification was not eased by my invariable response: "He got me down in the water out on the jetty and pretty near got away."

It was during another norther that my favorite duck story had its inception. I was hunting near High Island one day with the two Gonzales boys, Alcie and Bowie. We had risen at four o'clock in the morning, and, accompanied by a professional hunter who lived on High Island, had gone a distance of several miles through the woods to a stretch of open country dotted with small lakes and covered with marsh grass. The sun was about five to eight degrees high in the east and the sky was clear. Not a duck had we sighted.

Our hunter, a wise old chap, as if sensing our doubts upon this subject, remarked that we would see some ducks soon.

"I killed thirty-two mallards with one shot yesterday," he added.

Hardly had he spoken, when our horses' hoofs thundered on a small bridge. As though the sound were a signal, the entire prairie seemed to rise like a magic carpet. The whole atmosphere filled with wild ducks. They darkened the sun like a heavy cloudbank. Some flew a short distance to the southeast and lit.

Our hunter watched our eyes grow larger at the sight. Calmly pulling on his pipe, he remarked that we had ridden as far as we could along the route of lakes and mudholes. He volunteered to stay with the horses, adding, "You boys can go any way you wish. You will find ducks, plenty of them, wherever you go."

I had watched the fowl that had settled down toward the southeast, and now struck out in that direction. I had not gone far before I observed a small flock of ducks fly upward and alight not far away. I crept cautiously through the high marsh grass to the spot I took to be their resting place. Then I straightened up and took a look. Suddenly a mass of fowl arose, almost in my face, and where they had been flocking a large body of water was visible. The birds had been so densely packed upon its surface that the whole appeared to be solid ground. They were so close together that it seemed none could have moved unless all did.

As they were flying away from me, I sent two shots into the animated cloud. Ducks began to fall all around me. It literally rained ducks. I picked up as many as I could and started back toward the horses, leaving as many more crippled or dead upon the ground. Because of decimation by hunting and the diseases suffered by the wild game, I am certain that such numbers of brilliantly plumaged birds will never be seen again in the air at one time.

Those two shots and the incredibly large bag they netted me satisfied my hunting proclivities for the day. However, when we returned to our camp, we spied a flock of wild geese flying towards us from a northwesterly direction. Directing our guide's attention to them, we ducked into the long grass to await the coming of the flying game. Suddenly my companion relaxed, remarking in a somewhat rueful tone:

"It's no use. They're passing over too high. Your gun won't reach them."

"Let me try." I raised the barrel of my long-necked gun. When they were directly overhead, I pulled the trigger. A goose dropped out of the flock and fell to the ground.

I lowered my gun and turned triumphantly to my friend. "Watch the place where he fell, so that you can guide me to him." I tried to keep my voice matter-of-fact, but I could not help showing my exultation.

We began the search, my companion apparently rendered

wordless by the unexpected success of the shot. With some difficulty we located the bird in the thick, high grass, and returned with what was destined to be the only Canadian wild goose killed in the entire expedition. When the hunter next spoke, it was to offer to buy my gun. He explained that his English-made weapon was considerably outranged by it. It is needless to add that I was not interested in his proposal.

As I have remarked before, I have never seen birds in such profusion, unless it was in Tennessee when wild pigeons came in autumn to roost in the oak trees on my father's farm. These birds were so thick in acorn-time that it seemed to me they hid the tree-tops. A man I met who had been reared near Jasper, in East Texas, once verified this impression of vast numbers. He related that he had seen wild pigeons roosting, and that, when they were frightened into flight, the uppermost pigeons would break off limbs by their weight. He said these falling limbs killed pigeons roosting on the lower branches in greater numbers than he and his companions could carry away. He also took an oath that he had seen more than a wagonload of dead birds lying underneath a single tree. It is only right to add that considerable doubt was expressed by his hearers in regard to this part of the story.

With my brother and some other companions I often hunted plover both on Galveston Island and the mainland, ordinarily doing this type of hunting from a horse-drawn cart. I owned a fine dog that had been trained to jump down from the cart and retrieve the birds which we shot from our comfortable seats in the vehicle. With the words, "Go get him!" we would point out the spot where the birds had fallen, and the smart little beast invariably returned with everyone of them. On one occasion, however, this dog's faith in us was put to an acid test. While we were out shooting

near a lake at the lower end of the island, we crippled a
Mexican eagle, believing it to be a duck. The bird fell at
some little distance in the water. The pup made a quick
swim for it. Instead of his routine "fetch" he ran into a
vicious battle. Both contestants were bleeding profusely before we could call the dog away. In our opinions, the dog got
a little the worse of the battle.

Before turning to other subjects, just one more reference
to my sportsman's days in that fascinating hunting ground.

Isaac and I had gone fishing on Pelican Island across the
Bay with the son of a Baptist pastor. We had our lunch
with us (including several watermelons) and were seining
from a rowboat, when we ran upon an oyster reef. We took
a barrel out upon the reef, filled it with oysters still in their
shells, and transported the barrel ashore. Then we roasted
the oysters over a fire built on the spot.

The believe-it-or-not part of the story comes now. We
ate the entire barrel of roasted oysters—just the three of us.

With a climate ideally suited to the enjoyment of outdoor
affairs, the Galveston youth was devoted to such diversions
as oyster roasts, boat sails, fishing parties and hay rides, as
well as the more formal type of entertainments. I received
my full share of invitations, being a frequent visitor to palatial homes like those of the Stewarts, Garnetts, and other
leading Galveston families who possessed charming daughters. I also attended festivities given by the residents of
Hitchcock, between Galveston and Houston. On these occasions I met many members of the Galveston younger set,
who were accustomed to gather there on Sunday afternoons
and evenings.

At one time I was asked to bring some of my young
Hitchcock acquaintances to a sail and fishing party. At
the last moment, the young man who had planned the party
and rented the sailboat was called out of town. He notified

me that the plans for the party were off. I told him that, as I had already sent out the invitations, I would pay for the boat and be the host of the sail. I prevailed upon him to call the others and tell them that the affair was canceled. I then called three of the girls who were to have gone, re-invited them, and asked them to select their own guests.

The girls (all good friends of mine) were the daughters of a banker, the general passenger agent of a large railroad system, and a prominent physician. I had been lavishly entertained by all of them. With these young ladies as sponsors, I felt that the party would be a success, and it was. Although I found it the most expensive entertaining I had ever undertaken, I was both proud and pleased at the result.

It was through such social activities that I met the girl who was afterward to become my wife—the girl who was to be, from then on, the one girl in the world for me. Being a non-drinker, I was considered a desirable escort for the young people who came to enjoy the beauty of Galveston Beach. The wife of Dr. Lamar, pastor of a leading Baptist Church in Galveston at the time, chose me to be the exclusive escort of her niece during the latter's visit to her home.

The meeting which was to change the entire course of my life was brought about in a casual way. I was invited to a party at the home of Mrs. Cora Behrends, the mother of my friend Earl Behrends, who was afterward an employee of the Internal Revenue Collector's office at Dallas. Mrs. Behrends told me that she had also invited Miss Ula Jackson, a dear friend of hers and "the sweetest girl in Texas," as she phrased it.

"But don't get ideas and fall in love with her," she warned me in a joking way. "I understand she is already engaged."

In the same bantering vein, I replied with proper gallantry, "That only makes the prospect of meeting her more interesting." I further informed Mrs. Behrends that I had

heard much about her paragon from other people, and could
hardly wait for our meeting.

That night, as I entered the Behrends home, escorting
another young lady, I saw Miss Jackson leaving the dressing
room to mingle with the other guests. At the first sight of
her I drew a long breath. Slim, vivacious—rose-and-white
skin—a kindly spirit shining through eyes as grey as the
waters of her own island birthplace. A sudden thought took
possession of me. One idea filled my whole universe: That
is the girl I want. After such an experience, nothing can
shake my belief that when a man meets the one girl he desires, he is instantly aware of it.

A few nights later I called upon her. On that evening I
told her I had met the girl I was going to marry. Perhaps
she understood, as women have a way of doing. Or perhaps
she meant it when she told me afterward she thought I was
referring, in that statement, to the girl whom I had escorted
to the Behrends party. In any event, any misunderstanding
that might have existed was soon cleared up. To be more
definite, the lovely Miss Jackson (who had not been engaged at all) became very much engaged—and to me.

All this took place only a few weeks before the devastating
hurricane of 1900. Before that catastrophe, Galveston was a
delightful place in which to live, and possessed a lotus-eater
charm for the visitors. Its streets and avenues were arranged
with alphabetical precision. Its long, wide thoroughfares
were lined with the palatial homes of millionaires, and were
bordered with red and white oleanders. Unexpected turns in
the road revealed a white beach strewn with gleaming oyster
shells, and a breath-taking glimpse of blue sea that shone in
the background. The business portion of the town presented
a more commercial aspect. Numerous small grocery stores,
located in the suburbs, sold fish and beer and did a rushing
business. There was always a crowd of visitors around the

network of glittering spars, especially in the vicinity of the wharf. Some big ship would arrive from a foreign port every few hours. A transport would dock. The air would be filled with the raucous cries of dark-eyed, barefooted sailors unloading a banana boat. To these, as an accompaniment, was added the ceaseless clop-clop of the sullen, dark green water against the boats and beneath the jetties. During the summer the beach was always lined with people sight-seeing. This was a beautiful sight to behold, with the rolling and splashing waves as a background.

The exotic charm of the atmosphere, and the warmth and color of a semitropical climate were reflected in the character and actions of the Galvestonians. There was a mingling of every nationality; the people of Galveston all seemed like members of one big and happy family. Rich and poor, high and low, meeting on the streets, at the beach, or in public places, hailed each other as friends. Yet all this brightness, beauty and happiness were to be swiftly blotted out by the dark shadow of a terrific hurricane. This forced many other people, as well as myself, to depart from the "Happy Hunting Grounds" of Galveston.

CHAPTER IV

THE GALVESTON HURRICANE

On September 7, 1900, a tropical hurricane was reported moving in across the Gulf from Cuba. The signs pointed to its crossing Florida and continuing up the Atlantic Coast, but it suddenly changed course, veering westward through the Gulf. All that day (Friday) I remained busy distributing information as to the storm's movements. By Friday night the disturbance was central-southwest of New Orleans, moving westward. I prepared and issued a weather map and deposited it in the post office about midnight, for the morning train to the Texas interior. Afterward, I went to the home of my brother, Dr. Isaac M. Cline, a distance of about a block from the Gulf, and to my room there. I went to bed about one o'clock, and fell into a fitful and restless slumber, with the hurricane still pressing heavily upon my mind.

About four o'clock in the morning, I awoke, filled with a sense of impending disaster. In some obscure way, I sensed that the waters of the Gulf were already over our back yard. One glance out of the south window facing the Gulf showed me that my presentiment was correct. I immediately awoke my brother and told him that the worst had begun. We reached an immediate agreement and decided upon our division of labor. I was to assemble data for a message about the tide for the seven o'clock observation, which was scheduled to go out over the Weather Bureau circuit to the nation. He was to remain on the beach, warning people back to higher ground and keeping me advised as to the movements of the tide.

Later while I was temporarily in charge, giving out all

weather information, a railroad conductor came to the office and asked my advice about his train's departure. I told him he had better join his family and take them somewhere near the center of the city.

He said, "I am going to take that train out of here at one o'clock in the afternoon."

I replied, "All trains stopped running hours ago. All tracks down the island leading to Houston are under water. You won't take any train out of Galveston for several days."

All day long Saturday the water kept rising, with the barometer increasing the speed of the instrument's fall and the wind growing in force. At 3:30 p. m., 75th m. t., I took a special observation to be wired to the Chief at Washington. The message indicated that the hurricane's intensity was going to be more severe than was at first anticipated. About this time, my brother paused in his warnings long enough to telephone from the beach the following fact, which I added to the message: "Gulf rising rapidly; half the city now under water." Had I known the whole picture, I could have altered the message at the time of its filing to read: "Entire city under water."

The speed of the water's rise continued to increase. By the time I had completed and enciphered the message, all Galveston was inundated. The entire pavement of wooden blocks throughout the business section was afloat and up to the level of the raised sidewalks, bobbing up and down like a carpet of corks. I waded through the swirling water knee-deep in places to file the wire, breaking through the floating pavement at each step—a highly difficult mode of progress. After struggling through to the Western Union office, I learned that the wires had been down for two hours.

I waded a block farther, to the Postal Telegraph Office. Again my message was refused, with the statement that it would be impossible to send it. Their wires, too, had been down for a similar length of time. I made my way painfully back again, through the top crust of wooden blocks, to the Weather Bureau. I called the office of the Telephone Company, and asked for a long distance connection with the Western Union at Houston, at the utmost speed. The operator refused to connect me, informing me that there were more than four thousand calls ahead of mine. She stuck to her refusal even after I told her that the telegraph wires were down, and that I had a vital "rush" Government message which took precedence over all types except news of death.

In desperation, I asked for the manager, Mr. Tom Powell. Much to my relief, he was there, and I explained to him the urgent nature of my need—delivery of the contents of my message to the Chief at Washington. I filed the message, at the same time requesting officials at the telegraph office to treat as confidential the news it contained—that Galveston was wholly submerged by the flood. The two cities, Galveston and Houston, were traditional rivals. I explained that the facts in the message were the property of the Weather Bureau and of the Government, and were not for public release except from Washington.

After I had sent the telegram, I felt that I had done all I could at the Bureau. I then asked Mr. John D. Blagdon, an observer, to remain in the office to handle anything that might come up, telling him that it was unlikely that he would receive any more telephone calls. I had decided to go to the beach and join in sounding the alarm of the imminent peak of the blow. I also wished to persuade more people to go to the center of the town for safety. I chose the beach on the Gulf side of the city, in order to be as near as possible to my brother's house, and to aid the occupants there should they need assistance. The house was so strongly built that it had withstood the worst of all previous storms.

I waded in overflow waters for more than a mile, yelling to people along the route that the worst was yet to come and calling on them to get to the city's center if they could. In my judgment, the wind's velocity was, at that time, between sixty and one hundred miles an hour. I passed the Sherwood place, about two blocks from the beach. I was in time to see the family set forth for the Catholic Convent, where they would have been safe. They never reached their destination, lost later in the rising tide. I was frequently blown several feet out of my way by gusts of high winds.

When I reached my brother's sturdily constructed house on the beach, standing there like a lighthouse built upon a rock, I found that he had arrived at his home in safety. He was at the bedside of his wife, who was expecting a little one before long, and who was then ill. He could not move her, for, even if they were able to reach a safer place, exposure to the raging elements might have meant her death. Had it been otherwise, she and the entire family would have been long ago sheltered in the city's center, instead of directly in the path of the storm on the unprotected shore. When I arrived, the water was waist-deep in places near the house and in the streets, making escape virtually out of the question. Indeed, many of the people to whom I had shouted a warning as I made my way to the beach were killed by flying debris, or drowned. The homes on the beach, from which the occupants had been unwilling to flee, were blown down and submerged, or washed away.

I called my brother outside to discuss the situation, so as not further to alarm those within the house. While we were weighing the chances for and against getting away in safety, the wind shifted from north to northeast. At the same time, the water made a startling rise of about four feet in as many seconds, eliminating the last chance of wading to safety. We re-entered the house, a two-story structure, and the water

crept in after us a few minutes later. It finally drove us upstairs, and, at last, we were all gathered in one room selected
for its location on the windward side, so that we should be
on the top wall of the building as it would fall if blown over.
I told the others that I believed the house would go, as this
storm would be more severe than any hurricane that had
ever struck Galveston Island.

Nearly fifty persons, including whole families of neigh-
bors, had sought refuge in my brother's house. The contractor who built it was there among them. He knew, better
than anyone, that its construction was of the finest and
strongest materials, as my brother intended it to withstand
the worst wind that ever blew. Until my statement of the
danger, everyone there had believed it to be immune to
destruction by storm.

At dark on that fateful day of September 8, 1900, the
black desolation of which will forever live in my memory,
the house was still standing. Surrounding it were scenes of
ruin and destruction, every house in sight having gone to
pieces. Even before dark came, homes and wreckage of
homes drifting past into the whirling chaos had torn away
from my brother's house the two-story porches at the front
and rear. The water had attained a depth of perhaps fifteen
feet. Strangely enough, amid the seething turmoil, I did not
feel unduly excited. In fact, I was almost calm. I was convinced that, in some way or another, I should come out of it
alive. I kept thinking of an uncle of ours, who, alone of
all those aboard a sinking ship, saved himself by getting
on a plank when the vessel went under, and drifting upon
this frail support five miles to shore.

Again, as strongly as I could, I warned my relatives and
friends that the house was about to collapse. I urged them,
if possible, to get on top of the drift and float upon it when
the dangerous moment came. As the peril became greater, so

did the crowd's excitement. Most of them began to sing; some of them were weeping, even wailing; while, again, others knelt in panic-stricken prayer. Many of them were scrambling aimlessly about, seeking what, in their fright, appeared to be vantage points.

Then—it happened. The building could be felt moving from its foundation, blown over, or pushed by the current, slowly upon its beams. I had taken my position near a window on the windward side, and, as the house capsized, I seized the hand of each of my brother's two children, turned my back toward the window, and, lunging from my heels, smashed through the glass and the wooden storm shutters, still gripping the hands of the two youngsters. The momentum hurled us all through the window as the building, with seeming deliberation, settled far over. It rocked a bit and then rose fairly level on the surface of the flood.

The two youngsters and I were alone on the top side.

Not another human figure was to be seen on the drift. All the other occupants of that room, nearly fifty men, women and children, it appeared, were still trapped inside, for the house had not yet broken up. It still held together, in spite of the severe strain upon it. There was no means of egress except the window through which I had smashed my way into the clear. It was raining in torrents, and through winds of terrific force came flying pieces of timber. The clouds had broken in spots, and the dim light of the moon made it possible to see for a short distance over the mass of drift about us. It also enabled us to see more clearly that none of those who went under with the house had succeeded in reaching the unsubmerged wall. The latter, on which we were crouching, alternately rose and fell, first a few feet above the rushing tide, then down almost to the black whirling water.

The children were clinging to me for protection from the wind and the flying debris. I put them gently aside for a moment and lowered the top part of my body between the casings of the window which I had broken. I cupped my mouth with my hands and called into the room as loudly as possible: "Come here! Come here!" No answer came from the black depth beneath me. I had heard that the drowning would seize and cling to any object within reach. I lowered my legs through the window frame, letting them swing back and forth and around in the water as the house swung in its rocking movement. I had hoped that some of the trapped ones within the room might catch my feet and so be pulled out. My efforts were wasted and I finally gave them up. I have no words to tell the agony of heart I experienced in that moment.

Little by little the house had been breaking up. In spite of the added danger that lay in this development, my heart suddenly leaped with uncontrollable joy. In two figures that clung to the drift about one hundred feet to leeward, I discovered my brother and his youngest child. In some miraculous manner they had escaped alive from the house of doom. Only the mother, one of the dearest of women, was gone. We were never to see her alive again.

After the joy of our reunion, my brother explained how he came to be still alive. When the house overturned, he lost consciousness for a few moments, but was revived by the water pouring over him. Believing his entire family lost, he would gladly have died there, too, but in groping aimlessly about, he had brushed against his five-year-old daughter. Holding her tightly to him and exerting a strength born of desperation, he made a battle in her behalf against death by drowning. Before exhaustion overtook him, the disintegration of the building had begun, and, as one of the walls was breached, he had clung to some of the timbers, and clambered out with his child on top of a section of planking.

Our little group now numbered five. We remained close together, climbing and crawling from one piece of wreckage to another, with each of the latter in turn sinking under our weight. At one time it seemed as though we were indeed lost. A weather-battered hulk that had once been a house came bearing down upon us, one side upreared at an angle of about forty-five degrees, at a height from six to eight feet higher than our drift. The huge derelict was sweeping beneath it everything that lay in its path. I was conscious of being direly frightened, but I retained sufficient presence of mind to leap as the monster reached us, and to get a grip with my hands on the highest edge of the wreck. My weight was enough to drag it perceptibly lower in the water, and I called my brother, who added his weight to my own. Together we were able to pull the upper side downward and we climbed thankfully on the top with the children, just as the drift upon which we had been floating went to pieces under our feet.

For three hours, from eight to eleven, we floated on a multitude of drifts, by turns. We were swept out to sea for such a distance that finally we could see no lights anywhere. Suddenly, however, the wind became southerly, indicating that the storm's center was bending to northward, and our courses turned landward again. We finally floated back—sufficiently close to shore for the light to reappear, far to the north, but still comfortably visible. On a fairly substantial support for the time being, we braced ourselves in sitting positions with our backs to the wind, holding broken pieces of plank behind our heads to protect ourselves from flying missiles. When we could manage it, we sheltered the children, to some extent, between our legs. We learned later that many others like us, who had sought a precarious shelter on the top of drifts, had been killed by the flying timbers and other objects.

At one point, two other castaways, a man and a woman, joined us on the wreckage that, at that time, was serving us as a lifeboat. The strangers remained with us for some little time, until the man crawled up to where I sat, pulled the two children away, and tried to shelter himself behind my body. I pushed him indignantly away and drew the children back. He repeated the unspeakable performance. This time I drew out a knife that I carried, and threatened him with it. I warned him that I would use it on him if he attempted such an action again. I did not have it in my heart to put my threats into execution, nor to do him any injury. I was only protecting my brother's children from an individual who appeared to be drunk or temporarily bereft of his sanity. I felt that he was as well able to look after himself as the rest of us were to see to ourselves.

Then occurred a coincidence which I can not explain except as the merest chance. I can almost believe to this day that animals have superhuman senses in time of danger. A fine retriever hunting dog of mine, the pet of the family, somehow found us out of the storm—almost certainly, I repeat, by accident. Yet there he was in the maelstrom, clawing his way up to our drift and upon it, and dashing about to smell each one of us, then tearing across to the edge, apparently in search of the children's mother. I believe he was determined to seek her, wherever she was in those wild waters. At any rate, his intention to leave us was obvious, and I called him back. When he ignored my shout, poising on the edge preparatory to leaping back into the sea, I made a lunge for him, but he dodged, outran me, and plunged over the side of our drift. We never saw him any more.

Suddenly I became aware of the taste of salty blood in my mouth, mingling with raindrops trickling down my face and over my lips. Putting my hand to my head, I discovered that a long gash had been cut in my scalp. Though I had felt no blow, I was sure that the wound had occurred when I smashed through the window as the house went over. Oddly enough, there was never any pain, even after a considerable time had passed. I was numb to any sensory feeling for days after the storm.

We had to keep moving from one insecure float to another, as each went to pieces. By now we had floated back into the southern edge of the city, and, for the first time, could hear cries for help. The calls were coming from a large, two-story house standing directly in the path of the drifting mass which we had made our latest refuge. Apparently the occupants believed we were coming from the Gulf in a boat. Next moment our mass struck the house, demolishing it and no doubt scattering the inhabitants into the water and the darkness.

My brother was struck and knocked down by one of the hurtling timbers, and all my attention was directed to him. I found, to my relief, that he was not badly hurt. After he was on his feet again, I noticed a little girl struggling in the water. Under the impression that she was my brother's youngest child, I managed to catch her garments before she floated out of reach. I set her upon the drift with the rest of us. She was smaller than the other two, and, still believing she was my niece who had been washed overboard when her father was hurt, I placed her beside me for greater safety.

As we floated toward the city, the light grew brighter. Our drift began to open into holes, which often closed quickly again as the timbers worked back and forth. The oldest child fell into one of these, and I had barely caught her up from the watery void before it closed again. I thrust her back into safety, but she called to her father in a panic: "Papa! Papa! Uncle Joe is neglecting Rosemary and me for this strange child!" For the first time I looked closely at the little girl I had fished out of the water some time before. I then glanced over my shoulder at my brother. He was still bending protectively over his baby. The child I had rescued, therefore, was not my niece but a stranger. I kept her with the other two at my side until we reached the point from which a light was shining. It was a house and it was on solid ground.

In that building, surrounded by wreckage, we made our landing about one hour before midnight. Tired and unspeakably battered, we climbed through an upstairs window into a room from which the roof and ceiling had been blown away. Just under the floor of the room, the black waters of the Gulf were lapping. After having fought a frantic battle of body and mind for three hours, we dragged ourselves wearily inside. We found there a huddled group of people who told us that the water was falling—had dropped about a foot from its flood peak. At any rate, we had something solid beneath our feet again, and in that room we thankfully rested the remainder of that Saturday night. By Sunday morning the storm waters had retreated into the Gulf again, and the long siege was over.

As we emerged, grateful to be alive, dreadful sights met our gaze on all sides. From the time we descended the stairs to make our way to the home of some acquaintances in the city's center area, we climbed over dead bodies sprawled and piled where the flood had left them, and over heaps of wreckage. Debris from four to ten feet deep and extending for blocks packed with dead was all that was left of thousands of homes and the human beings who had lived in them just one day earlier. Sand had obliterated the streets and the lots. The inevitable looting had already begun. We had made our way only four blocks when we observed pilferers at work on bodies and possessions, on that morning which, ironically enough, was the Sabbath. I even came upon some thieves breaking into my own trunk, which had washed far from what had once been my home. I stopped this process long enough to take out a few things I especially valued, and then continued on my way, leaving the rest of its contents to the looters.

Viewed from the top of mountainous wreckage, the residential section of a city which had been the home of over thirty-five thousand people was merely a desolate waste. Not a house was left standing in the area ravaged by the flood, nor could a single street be outlined by the eye. The exact number of the dead was never known, because so many of the bodies were washed away. At least five thousand corpses were eventually recovered, however, and were either buried or burned. The best figure available placed the fatalities from various causes, at more than eight thousand.

We learned that thousands of survivors had undergone ordeals similar to our own. As for me, I was compelled to begin life over again after the storm. My sole possessions were the remains of the clothing in which I had spent that terrible night, and a lot situated near the center of the ravaged residential section.

My brother's beloved wife was the only one of his family missing. She, and most of the others who were trapped in that room together, never escaped from the waters. Twenty days later her body was found and identified by her diamond engagement ring. We laid her to rest in the Galveston cemetery.

Later I met Mr. Powell, Bell Telephone executive, who had so signally aided me in forwarding my message to Washington. I thanked him again for his assistance in that undertaking. He told me that, at the time my call was put through, only a single wire still connected Galveston and Houston, and that one broke almost simultaneously with the end of my conversation. It happened in this way that my message was the last one of any sort carried from the stricken city for several days. The Chief of the Weather Bureau wrote an article in the September, 1927, issue of the *American Mercury*, commending me for getting the final message out on that momentous occasion so long ago. He recalled that the message had stressed the need for relief, and predicted that "great destruction of life must ensue." The article went on to say that it was an act of vision, and that "probably no man will ever render such noble service for humanity" as I did at Galveston "during that awful catastrophe."

The strange child that I had lifted out of the drift proved to be the seven-year-old daughter of parents whose home was in San Antonio, where her father was employed in a large department store. I left her in charge of the people living in the house wherein we had "landed," first inquiring her name and learning that her entire family, with the exception of her father, was in Galveston. I intended to list these facts with the newly established rescue board. I left her weeping bitterly at being parted from her new-found friend, but safe and in good hands.

Some days later, still shaken and ill from the experience of that dreadful night, I entered a drugstore to buy some medicine. A grief-stricken man stood at the counter in earnest conversation with the druggist. I overheard him say he was living in San Antonio. Acting upon a sudden impulse, I drew nearer and asked him if he knew a little girl called Cora Goldbeck.

I shall never forget his face, lined with dread and horror, as he replied, "She is my daughter."

"Then your daughter is safe," I told him. I then gave

him an account of the lucky accident by which I had saved her from the flood.

His face transformed with relief, the man threw his arms around me, repeating in a choking voice, over and over "My God! Cora! My Cora!" When his emotion had in some measure subsided, he wanted to be taken to her immediately. I explained that Galveston was under martial law and that it was not possible to get to the beach that night. I added quickly, however, that I had a pass that would take us through the military lines at any time next morning.

In the course of our conversation, he told me that, during the three days he had been in Galveston frantically trying to trace the members of his family, he had been sleeping at the city hall. I took him with me, for the night, to the home in which I, myself, was being granted shelter; and he slept there on the floor. Next morning, as we hastened down Tremont Street on our way to the house where his child was staying, we came in sight of the Gulf, drowsing after its display of murderous violence. He stopped, raised his clenched fists and shook them, and, in a fit of fury, cursed the now subsiding water. He had never learned the fate of his family except in the case of the little girl. A few minutes later, however, his face wearing a very different and indescribably tender look, he took that one child in his arms.

Many years later, a sequel to this episode brought great happiness to my wife and to me. Miss Cora Goldbeck, a young lady of nineteen, visited us in our home at Corpus Christi, where she had come in person to thank me for saving her life. The lovely little girl had become a beautiful young woman.

Some time after the storm I was in conversation with a group of business men as talk turned to the future. Most of the group predicted that the city would never be rebuilt. My gift of prophecy was still strong, however, when I reminded them that Galveston was the only large city on the Gulf Coast west of New Orleans.

"It will be rebuilt," I told them. "Commerce always takes precedence over life."

My words were to become true. From the desolation wrought by wind and sea, a new city emerged—no longer a starry-eyed maiden with oleander blossoms in her hair, but a grief-tempered, self-reliant woman. It is history that a great and prosperous Galveston rose from the ruins of that storm-wrecked island. But, as I wrote in an earlier chapter, it was never quite the same. The wind of progress, as well as the wind from the Gulf has blown away many friendly aspects of the old days there.

The city did take to heart at least one lesson taught by the storm. It was remarked that the walls of the drift piled high on the south side of the city had afforded a great measure of protection for the central portion of the town, and a safeguarding sea wall eventually went up at that exact point.

Language and photographs are unable to portray the horror and destruction wrought by the 1900 hurricane. Even today, when I think of it, my heart bleeds and the tears fall from my eyes. As the storm curved in its course and passed inland toward Houston, it diminished in intensity, because of contact with the rigid earth's surface. Notwithstanding this, several thousand people were killed on the mainland to the north of Galveston.

Some of the sights and freakish occurrences noted after the storm were almost unbelievable. It was reported from the mainland area that a woman, struggling to escape from the rapidly rising water, crawled under a barbed-wire fence that barred her way, after she had failed to climb over. Days and days later, she was found, her long hair caught in the barbed wire. Her hands were still clutching her hair, indicating that she had died endeavoring to disentangle it.

CHAPTER V

AUTHOR'S TRIP TO PORTO RICO

The Galveston storm was to have a shattering effect on my physical health for a long time to come. In fact, even now, although I am past seventy, I have never ceased to realize that I might have been a stronger man, had it not been for that experience of shock and exposure—and for that which was to occur to undermine further my native good health in a subsequent assignment to the tropics.

Immediately after the hurricane I was called to Washington to render a personal report to Professor Willis L. Moore, Chief U. S. Weather Bureau. On my way, I made a stopover visit to my parents in Tennessee. I received a letter from an assistant at the Galveston Weather Bureau, a man named Nichols, who had worked with me. He paid me the compliment, in his letter, of informing me that he had told the official in charge it would take two men to fill my shoes even to a partial extent, during my absence from my post there.

In the National Capital, after I had reported to my Chief, he informed that I was to receive a promotion, as Section Director of Porto Rico. I expressed appreciation of this recognition granted my work, but produced a letter from my physician, Dr. Truehart, in Galveston, giving an account of the weakened condition in which my experience on that terrible night of the storm had left me. The doctor's report said that I would certainly be susceptible to the "native fever" of the island—a tropical malaria—then so prevalent in the Caribbean area. It was true my health was most uncertain. I was barely out of bed, my lymphatic glands were swollen to an abnormal size, and I was in great need of a prolonged rest.

Professor Moore told me that he understood the circumstances, but explained that the Weather Bureau was having trouble in Porto Rico. "We feel that any man who could do what you did at Galveston," said he, "can straighten out the situation down there. If you should get the fever there, write me personally and I will bring you back to this country at once."

I felt that his appeal left me no alternative, and accepted the assignment. A letter was furnished from the President of the United States, designating me as special envoy, to be presented to the Governor General when I reached Porto Rico. In December, 1900, I left Washington and proceeded to my new post, where I called upon the Governor General, accompanied by my first assistant, G. Harold Noyes. The Governor General read the letter carefully, and, making no immediate reference to it, engaged me in a casual conversation for about thirty minutes. Then he seemed to arrive at a decision.

"Dr. Cline," he said, "I appreciate your coming. After talking with you, I can assure you that we will get along nicely together. There will be no trouble in the future."

I thanked him for his kindness and asked him to call on me for any assistance I might be able to furnish. The interview was over.

This ended the long-standing friction between the Governor General and the United States Weather Bureau there. It seemed that my predecessor in the office and the Governor General could not agree. The closing of office quarters for the Weather Bureau was being considered. The feud had been in the nature of a minor international complication.

This conflict disposed of at the very beginning, I believe I achieved all that had been hoped for in sending me there.

I established several co-operative meteorological stations at scattered points over the island, one at the exact highest point of land, El Yunke, a city on the loftiest mountain range in Porto Rico, situated 3,609 feet above the sea and overlooking the entire island. I also completed the first study of nomenclature of all crops grown, an article which was afterward reprinted in the Monthly Weather Review at Washington, and reproduced in several European publications.

I went outside my official duties to solve yet one more problem which had been sorely baffling the island officials —the mystery of the "suicide week-ends."

Mr. Sleeper, the Governor General's private secretary, and I had become warm friends. He frequently called to see me and to discuss at length the affairs of administration. One Monday night, after publication in the day's paper of one of these unaccountable suicides, the topic came up in our conversation. Nearly every Monday paper in preceding weeks for several months had published a similar story. They were accounts of suicides by members of the Governor General's local National Guard, a native outfit quartered immediately across the street from his mansion and about one block from my office. I asked Mr. Sleeper the reason for these suicides.

"I only wish I knew," he said. "The seeming lack of any cause has given both the Governor General and myself great concern."

"Wait a moment," I said, a thought that had been in the back of my mind pushing its way forward and giving me an inkling of the cause of the mystery. "Didn't the newspapers say, in each instance, that the man who killed himself had been on kitchen police duty?"

After a moment's thought, Mr. Sleeper said he believed that had been true in each case. "I believe that the solution is right there," I told him. "These boys, with their keen native pride, feel disgraced in the eyes of their friends at being assigned to menial labor."

Then I told him about my janitor, who had been on the verge of starvation at the time I employed him. Yet, one day, when I instructed him to go out and clean the balcony floor in plain view of the people in the street, he refused, indicating that he could never face again those who chanced to see him engaged in that type of work.

Mr. Sleeper's eyes were opened immediately. He looked keenly at me a moment, slapped his knee, and said, "I believe you've hit it."

"I'm certain that is the answer," I replied. "Find some method of punishment other than kitchen police duty for your guards and see if the suicides don't come to an end."

My advice was put into practice, and the outcome was as I had foreseen. There was no more self-destruction in the ranks. Thereafter, the Governor General's secretary made a point of consulting me as to any course of action under consideration, giving me a standing with the island's administrator that made possible my obtaining the latter's authority for virtually anything I wished.

Washington seemed vastly pleased with all these achievements. Professor Moore had decided to put into effect an earlier suggestion of mine that the first Weather Bureau forecast center in the South be established at New Orleans. The new regional station was scheduled to be opened on July 1, 1901. In another departure from the old order, the Texas Section was due to be transferred from Galveston to Houston. Professor Moore had planned for me to return and take charge of the latter.

But, after all, I had contracted the "native fever." My health was temporarily gone; and, when I arrived at the boat at San Juan to return to the United States, I had to be assisted on board. My friends did not believe that I should live to disembark at New York. I was returning under the doctor's orders to go home and recuperate in a suitable climate. So Professor Moore changed his plans and assigned me to a resort city, Sandusky, Ohio, where I was placed in charge of the local Weather Bureau Office.

My naturally strong constitution reasserted itself, and I was soon able to go to work again, but I had not recovered sufficiently to assume the responsibility of the state center at Houston. There was relatively little work attached to my convalescent post, since all weather maps were printed in Cleveland and forwarded daily to Sandusky for distribution. I had an assistant able to take observations and perform other routine duties adequately, leaving me time for writing, study, and rest. Among other achievements, I wrote an article on Porto Rico which was published in the Monthly Weather Review.

I continued to regain strength with increasing rapidity, though I was not, for years to come, destined to recover from the effects of the storm. Nevertheless I had made such rapid strides towards recovery that my fiancée and I were enabled to set the date for our marriage for the month of December, 1901.

Lecture on Porto Rico

At this point, I am reprinting in full an address on the subject of Porto Rico, delivered at the Galveston Young Men's Christian Association at the request of my good friend, Dr. Palmer, the Y. M. C. A. secretary, who had asked me to speak when I should be again in the city. As I felt myself to be under great obligations to him at this time, I wrote him in return that I would make the address, entitled "My Trip to Porto Rico," which was as follows:

Before beginning my lecture, I wish to say that it is the greatest pleasure of my life to be back in Galveston and see so many of the old friends who weathered along with me the awful storm of September, 1900.

Did it ever seem to you that life is, after all, only an intelligent existence in a world which is just a big theater's stage? And that every human being is an actor or an actress, taking part in an order of events possessing dramatic unity and interest, and going to make up the welfare and happiness of every person on this lovely earth?

This, at any rate, was the thought which passed through my mind when, in December a year ago, I left the United States to take up my residence in the West Indies—the trip of which my appearance before you tonight is the result—and it returns again to me now as I am about to outline to you the details of my journey to, and stay in, our new possession. I refer to Puerto Rico, whose name was changed by act of Congress to Porto Rico.*

At the time I was stationed here in Galveston, and it was from this storm-swept city that I set forth. I passed around the base of Lookout Mountain, at Chattanooga, Tennessee, where the Confederate and Union armies fought a battle above the clouds. My trip was in the fall, after the first killing frost. The green leaves had taken on a crimson color and were having an outgoing party, bidding a farewell to the great forest trees. The latter were fast losing their summer green in anticipation of the cold north winds of winter.

As our train neared the tunnel at that point, the passengers were privileged to gaze upon noted battlefields of the North and South engagements. In the background were the rugged, jagged mountains and the dizzy, beetling cliffs, all alike clothed in dress of crimson and fading green. The mountains faced the beautiful verdant valley dotted here and there with areas of wild flowers whose lips, pearly with dew,

---

*By act of Congress, May 17, 1932, the official name of the island was changed back to Puerto Rico.

sparkled in the sunshine. The scene charmed the passengers' senses with its surpassing beauty, which was such as to gratify the esthetic faculties of the best judge of nature, art, or mind. Then we passed into the tunnel I have mentioned, which only a short distance in length, must have provided many, a memory to brides and grooms granted that moment of darkness and seclusion so soon after the exalting experience through which they had just passed. You need not blush for them. So many lovers must have delighted at passing through that tunnel.

Twelve days later I was in Washington, the Nation's Capital. There, I visited the Congressional Library, all of the public buildings, the zoo, and nearly every point of interest. I had the experience of being in the U. S. Senate Chamber when the message of the martyred President, William McKinley, was delivered to the Sixty-Sixth Congress.

After spending fifteen days in Washington, I continued my trip to New York, where I had five days before the scheduled sailing time. I visited "Dante's Inferno," Delmonico's, and other landmarks, strolling up and down Broadway among the skyscrapers. Of course, my sightseeing included that street of universal notoriety, the Bowery, the home neighborhood of Steve Brodie, who reputedly jumped off the Brooklyn Bridge. I understand that Steve, poor fellow, is no more. Another visit was to Canfield's great gambling hall. Jerome has had the police there since, but they are always late in saving a good man.

I boarded the S. S. *Philadelphia* on the morning of December 15, 1900, for Porto Rico. We were soon rounding Sandy Hook, opposite Rockaway Beach, and a few hours later were moving out to sea at a point east of Asbury Park. All of us were on deck, gazing anxiously back in farewell to the homeland, and wondering when we should return to it and our loved ones. Then night came, and, with it, dark clouds which gathered rapidly and thickly near the eastern horizon. Our ship speedily was rocking among mighty waves. A few hours later, the wind was blowing a gale. Fresh from my experience with the storm, the night, and the sea at Galveston, I slept rather badly. The sea became ever more furious and before dawn we were off Cape Hatteras, the most tempestuous and perilous point on the Atlantic Coast and the age-old nemesis of sailors. Every wave poured over the deck and not a passenger was permitted to leave his stateroom. Then, in the setting of the storm's majestic scene, I became what I never was during the Galveston hurricane on those housetops all but submerged in a raging flood—seasick.

As you probably have all been to sea, you know how comfortable and pleasant it is for the meal hour to come and nobody to be able to eat the repast prepared. A number of us were lining the rail, indulging the digestive whims of our interiors, when our captain happened by. He remarked to me that I appeared to have a weak stomach. I was miserable but game, and I responded, "Captain, I am doing as well as any of them."

In a few days, however, we had sailed into the warm ocean currents away southeast of Florida near the Bermuda Islands. Now we spent our time looking upon flying fish, pleasant days, and a calm sea. On the fifth day, the ship was ploughing along between the latitudes of 17° and 50' and 18° and 30' North, and longitude 65° and 30' and 67° and 15' west from Greenwich. We sighted land at a point east of the Mona Passage, which borders on Haiti, and excitedly debated whether we had discovered the smallest and easternmost island of the Greater Antilles. When we were told that the land we had seen was actually an island, we looked forward with eagerness to exploring it and achieving fame for the ship and crew. On coming nearer, however, we found our explorer's job blighted; that island had been discovered and explored, and the Stars and Stripes flew in the gentle breeze, extending a warm welcome. It was Porto Rico, one of our new possessions, and its discoverer was Columbus, on November 16, 1493, during his second voyage to the Western Hemisphere—quite a few days prior to our landing.

We are taught that Columbus first sighted Cape Mala Pascua and sailed along the south and east coasts to Aguada, where he landed November 19, 1493, to take possession of the island in the name of the reigning sovereign of Spain. He christened it San Juan Bautista, or St. John the Baptist. Its Indian name was Borinquen, or "the happy, unmolested hunting grounds."

For fourteen years after its discovery the island remained unexplored. Trading vessels stopped there occasionally, usually for water, but it was not until 1508 that Ponce De Leon made his landing from Santo Domingo and established a form of government other than that of the Indians. He founded the town of Caparra, about three miles inland from the Bay of San Juan, in 1509, and this town was afterward moved to the present site of San Juan and was named Porto Rico, or "Rich Gate." Subsequently, the island and the city exchanged names, and that point at which the first town was founded is now known as Pueblo Viejo, or "Old Town."

Porto Rico, by virtue of its situation, practically controls the Virgin and Mona passages from the Atlantic into the Caribbean Sea and occupies a strategic position of much importance—an importance that, subsequent events show, was recognized at an early date. Thus, in 1597, San Juan was blockaded and captured by Admiral George Clifford, Earl of Cumberland, but an epidemic of yellow fever forced him to give up the island. Two years before, San Juan had fallen before the assaulting forces of the great English sea rover, Sir Francis Drake. These conquests led to completion of San

Cristobal Castle, at the east end of the city of that name, and of Morro Castle, at the entrance to the harbor of San Juan. You will note that Porto Rico, as well as Cuba, has a Morro Castle, and I doubt if you ever heard the explanation. We say "Morro Castle," but in Spanish they use the word *Morro* only. I confess that for some time I did not know why each island belonging to Spain had a Morro Castle, but I learned that they so designated any fort with lighthouse attached at the largest port. These castles are eloquent, in their ancient and moss-grown dunes of rampart and battlement, of some of the most heroic and tragic chapters of human history. The walled castles were built from necessity, for no man in that Ishmaelitish age could live safely or peacefully save behind gun-fringed battlements sentineled night and day by sleepless eyes. The island was for more than a century menaced by prowling pirates, some of them more savage and cruel than was Drake himself. In addition to walling in San Juan, the capital, for protection from pirates, the Spaniards maintained deep ravines or trenches, easily flooded with water, outside the walls to block the onward march of an enemy.

The scenery here is reminiscent of the walled eastern cities of ancient times. As one stands near either castle and gazes eastward across the harbor over the low coast land, one sees in the distance an irregular range of low mountains and hills that traverses the island from east to west at a point a little south of its center. This range culminates in the peak El Yunke—"the Anvil" which overlooks the country from an altitude of 3,609 feet; it emerges majestically from the sea, with its retinue of associated but far lesser steeps lined up toward the west, and stands near the northeast corner. This range forms the water divide of Porto Rico, and is known by various names in different parts of the island, among them being Sierra de Cayey, Cordillera

Central and Sierra de Luquilla, the latter being in the northeast portion. Most of the interior has a steep, hilly surface, broken by deep ravines and creeks, which heavy tropical rains in some cases turn into unfordable rivers for a few hours' time. The largest streams are the Rios Loiza, Bayamon, Morovis, Arecibo, and Blanco, all situated on the north side of the Divide, and all navigable by small boats. Lying to eastward of Porto Rico and belonging to the United States are the small islands of Vieques and Culebra, named for the crab and snake, respectively.

The Porto Rico climate is not so oppressive as might be expected in its tropical situation. A cool, pleasant, and most welcome breeze generally blows across the island, particularly in the afternoon and at night, and this adds much to the comfort of the residents. Much cloudy weather prevails, with occasional fog in the mountains. Temperatures of 55 to 65 degrees Fahrenheit are considered cold in that latitude, especially by the poorly clad natives, who shrug their shoulders and sigh, "Mucho frio"—very cold. The so-called wet season usually begins in April and continues until December, the rainfall, whose annual average is from 54 to 134 inches, being greatest in the mountains.

Rains in this season are very sudden. You are walking down the street, under a brightly shining sun in a cloudless sky. Then, a minute or so later, you see a small, white, fleecy cloud, of no greater size than a dollar bill appeared to be in that country, prior to American occupation; and in another minute you are drenched by a heavy rainstorm. The effect is as if a winged figure had sped across the sky, squeezing out a large and exceptionally moist sponge; then the clouds disappear as though swept by a giant eraser, and the sun suddenly bursts forth as before. Many such rains may occur within a radius of two or three blocks—often on one side of a street while it remains dry and sunny on the other.

Only scattered remnants of the primeval forests are left, with the wooded areas small and mostly confined to the highest of the mountains. Timber is very scarce, and it is fortunate that very little is needed. Lumber for most of the buildings is imported. The island once was covered with mahogany, ebony, and sandalwood, but these valuable timbers were utilized or exported by the Spaniards, some say. Mr. J. W. Van Leenhoff, a friend of mine who owns a coffee plantation near Ysolina, Porto Rico, has a residence constructed of mahogany—a beautiful, red building adorning the mountainside, which would make a lovely home for any bride.

More than one-fifth of the island is under cultivation and crops yield well, considering the manner of their tillage. Hoeing done to free the ground of pernicious vegetation is usually performed with the machete, a long, heavy knife. Sugar, tobacco and coffee are the principal crops, but almost any product can be grown successfully. Oranges, bananas, and most tropical fruits grow without special cultivation, and the saying is that the island can raise anything—even good grafters. The answer returned to this was that virtually any product could also be raised in the United States, where grafting was also done, even the grafting of an apple to a peach. The ultimate illustration was advanced, in the story that it was a common occurrence to see, while proceeding along river bottoms, a pumpkin hanging on a rail fence.

The mountains, over portions of Porto Rico, are cultivated to their summits, and it is a pleasing sight to observe, while riding, a tiller of the soil with his machete at a point several hundred feet above you, where an animal could not make his way.

Transportation is very difficult. The French railroad now extends halfway around the western end of the island, but there are no other lines except a trolley connecting the beau-

Joseph L. Cline, Sectional Director, and two of his assistants visiting a coffee plantation in Porto Rico. Observe the native, with his mallet uplifted, husking coffee in the wooden urn.

tiful suburbs of Santurce with San Juan, the Capital. With the exception of the military wagon road constructed by the Spanish Government from San Juan to Ponce, there are no roads worthy the name but the roads built by the United States. Over most routes, pack trains comprise the only available mode of travel, and I passed some miserable days while trying to proceed by packsaddle along the mountain range. Once, near Barros, my horse fell with me, and I can visualize now the comical sight we must have made, horse and man, as the pair of us rolled down the mountainside together. My foot was caught in the stirrup, and I was like the Irishman who rolled down the hill strapped to the log—"By faith, on top half the time!" A few days later, I was bedridden by bruises and high fever, suffering so that death would have been a relief. In fact, I offered prayers that I might be permitted to die. Had the accident not befallen me, however, I might not have been here tonight, as I might have been kept stationed in Porto Rico.

While I was returning to San Juan later, I had an interesting lesson in the Spanish idiom. I called to see Dr. Chacar at Cayey. He was absent, but Señora Chacar met me at the door. I gave her my card, and she invited me in. I was to inspect there some meteorological records kept by her husband, who was my co-operative observer at that point. I asked her if she could speak English, and she answered, "No, Señor." Then I said, "Yo hablo poco Español" (I speak but little Spanish). After a short conversation in that language, she asked me what was the matter with my arm, which was in a sling. I answered, "Mi caballo caye con mi en campos cerca de Barros." She laughed very heartily at something which was obviously wrong in the Spanish sentence, and, on reaching my headquarters at San Juan, I asked my translator what it was. On hearing the sentence repeated, he, too, laughed, and refused to tell me the cause of his mirth—the

Spaniards are traditionally careful not to give offense to any one whom they like. After some persuasion, however, he informed me that I had misplaced my qualifying words, which, in Spanish, follow, not precede, the noun, as is the case in the German language. So I had given it the literal translation from English; I had thought I was saying, "My horse fell with me in the country near Barros." After I had finished persuading my rather embarrassed translator, using the final clinching argument that if I had said something wrong I wished to write an apology to Mrs. Chacar, I learned that, to a Spaniard, I had seemed to say "I was carrying the horse and fell." So I finally had a good laugh out of the affair myself.

It is common for Americans who have known only English to make grave mistakes when they first try to speak Spanish, on account of the peculiar construction of Spanish sentences. After my first month in the island, I took up my residence with a Spanish family, and there I was compelled to ask in their language for all my food. One day I asked for cold water, using the word "frito" instead of "frio," and found that I had requested "fried water;" and the ever-obliging waiter did bring me some heated water, which I suppose he had tried to fry.

The population is mixed, including whites, Negroes and Indians, with white strains predominating according to the census. There are 264 persons per square mile, the population's density being seven times that of Cuba and twice that of New York State. Spanish was the acknowledged language, but some spoke English, which was being taught in the public schools and was expected in time to be the dominant language —although I doubt it. The better class was well educated, highly civilized, and congenial, but few in number.

The lower classes accept witchcraft as a fact, belief in it being as prevalent as it was among the New England pio-

neers of this country over two hundred years ago. The super-
stition does not, however, reach the wide acceptance that it is
accorded in Jamaica, it is said, nor in Santo Domingo or
Haiti (where the standing of the white man compares with
the standing of the Negro in the southern portion of the
United States). Nor does witchcraft in Porto Rico have its
professional ministers, except that some persons are believed
to possess the "Evil Eye," which is undoubtedly a recognition of hypnotic power. I was walking down the street one
evening when I witnessed an instance of a little girl stricken
by an "Evil Eye." The child thought she was dying until a
second bystander said, "Quedo con Dios," which means
"God be with you." This broke the spell, whatever was its
nature, and the little girl recovered at once. But for this beni-
son, worded just as it was, the child might have died, or so
it was argued, of sheer terror. Many use charms and amulets
in warding off illness and trouble. I had my own, the left
hind foot of a graveyard rabbit, plucked at midnight by the
light of the moon, which was presented to me for luck by
a young woman in Washington prior to my departure. I am
sure it played a big part in averting the "Evil Eve" from me,
and I have that rabbit foot with me yet. You see, most people
do not know where to carry a rabbit's foot to get the maximum hoodoo effect. (At this point, I took the rabbit's foot
from the inside of my shoe.)

These amulets have been for so many generations the chief
aid in warding off and in curing sickness of all kinds that
some lower-class persons actually refuse medical treatment.
I knew of a man who was not expected to live who nevertheless refused medicine of any kind. His wife, however, took
charge of the medicine, administered it to herself, and sat
close by her husband's bed. When she returned to the doctor
next day, he inquired whether the medicine had helped her
husband. Her answer was, "Doctor, I took it and remained

as close to him as it was possible to get, but I am unable to see that he is better."

A common practice was to carry before the church altars silver images of the limbs, hands, body, or head, or other physical members affected by disease or pain. Here are two of the famous churches, that which was bombarded by Admiral Sampson, and that which is the oldest church edifice, built more than three hundred years ago. Some who have worshipped within its dingy walls may have looked upon Christopher Columbus in his Spanish prison chains. Here also is an altar said to be crowned with gold, the most costly shrine in the West Indies and equaled in value in few other lands.

The fertile island is covered with royal and date cocoanuts and with other palms, interspersed with lovely tropical flowers, ferns, and fruit plants of all descriptions, the whole comprising a grand and beautiful panorama. Beyond all lies the sea, which for twenty-eight out of thirty days on the average is a sleeping mass of purple topped by the sails of passing ships that reflect the twilight's golden sheen. Beyond the horizon lie more than a hundred other islands not so far away—empires of this storied part of the world. Those who sail beneath the guns of Morro Castle by Leper Island see a beautiful port, a haven, where mingled hues of sapphire and emerald glow and sparkle in the sunshine. The black hulls and yellow spars of the shipping and the white masses of steamers stand out like mosaics of jet, amber and ivory. Small wonder that the adventurous old Spaniard, whose daring prows had cut the stormy waters of many unknown oceans, found in these exquisite, tranquil coral seas the very ultima Thule of his wanderings and was led by his enthusiasm as he gazed on the picture, to bestow upon it the name Puerto Rico—"Rich Gate."

The island, under the Spanish regime, was to be likened

Typical country home of a native in Porto Rico (1901)

to the Garden of Eden about which we read in Holy Writ. Land which was not cultivated was tax-free, and was covered by wild-growing tropical fruits. The peons or the members of any class could gather this fruit and live without doing any sort of work; the food was there for the taking. To have made the Garden of Eden analogy complete, it would only have been necessary to give the name "forbidden fruit" to the silver, into which, by the way, the Government drilled holes so as to make it impossible to remove it from the island. The original forbidden fruit, reputedly the apple, was not to be found there.

San Juan, the capital, is a quaint, old-fashioned town, replete with the odd architectural examples, originating with the Conquistadores, that still survive among their descendants throughout the widely scattered possessions that fell under their conquering standards during the Fifteenth and Sixteenth Centuries. This architecture is a composite of what might be called the "Medievo-Mayan" styles, in which the prevailing modes of the Middle Ages of the Spanish Peninsula were blended with the massive and severe lines of the ancient Peruvians and Mexicans. With the latter, the conquerors had become familiar in occupying many pueblos, or villages, which they had overrun. It is a method of construction that cannot be improved upon for withstanding the force of earthquakes and hurricanes, though Porto Rico has never suffered to any great extent from either. An exception was a hurricane sustained in 1899. All buildings, excepting those of the peasant poor, which are of palms and wild grass, are built with thick stone or brick walls surmounted by huge beams serving as supports for flat roofs of brick or tiling. Until recently the buildings were only one story in height, but within the past few years the South American and West Indian cities have been gradually modernized, and three-story structures may be seen in many of them.

All other towns in Porto Rico are constructed on the pattern of San Juan, and the largest building in each is a church, centrally located. When it was wished to establish a town, a church was built first, the remainder of the city then growing up around it. None of the inland towns are nearly so modern as the Capital City, and many are not even entitled to have the word "town" applied to them. The streets of San Juan are all paved, usually with brick, and are well-lighted by gas and electricity. The city has a well-operated clubhouse, a public library, Young Men's Christian Association, water system, electric railway company, telephone system, and gas and electricity plants. It also has a history teeming with fire, blood, and pulsating human misery which marks a tragic chapter in time, and which is not exceeded in horror throughout the annals of this old world of ours.

The sea walls surrounding the city at a height of fifty to sixty feet and with a thickness ranging from ten to twenty feet are a majestic sight. They represent, however, ages of toil performed by Indian slaves under the stimulus of the lash. The Indians themselves, who once roamed at will over the picturesque island, no longer live to tell the tale. But their musical instruments survive them, including drums of various sizes made from the trunks of trees, the maracas, and the guicharo, made of the dried fruit of the calabash tree; and these instruments may be said to be the national tools of the island's music. They are still used for the dances of the Gibaros; and the guicharo, a long calabash shell with indentations, which is played upon with a stick, was used as an accompaniment to the piano and other modern instruments in society's balls. It was further adopted by Spanish military bands when they played for the country dances.

When I was welcomed to the island on my arrival, the leading part in this ceremony was taken by a party of natives with their crude musical instruments. I believe you would enjoy this music, and, in that belief, I have arranged to have a number played for you tonight by a native Porto Rican band. After it has been presented, I will display a number of articles typical of the unique features of life on the island.

(At this point, six youths, dressed in the costumes of the Porto Rican carnival season, took over an interval of the lecture, with an elaborate pantomime—much of which was grotesque to the audience's eye—instruction in which had previously been given them. This band, I believe, may lay claim to have introduced under my supervision, the use of what they now call "rattlers" and gourds which are used by the leading orchestras of the United States. My only son, Durward J. Cline, Sr., was the first orchestra leader in the United States to use these Porto Rican instruments for public dances.)

You have just heard a band really typical of Porto Rico, and you appeared to have enjoyed it. This is known as a "Carnival band," and, during the fiesta season, which gives the band its name, the natives go about in various forms of disguise. The hats these players wear are called "Los somberos de Carnival de Mayaguez." They are beautifully made by hand, woven in vari-colored grasses, and their cost on the island is only fifteen to twenty-five cents apiece, whereas in New York, where they are the current rage on Coney Island, they sell for five dollars each. At times other than Carnival, the bandsmen play their music in ordinary clothing.

I have already told you of the uses to which the guicharo, which you now see, is put. The tiplee is the prototype of a small American fiddle, and it is constructed of two pieces of wood. When it was first devised there was considerable uncertainty as to the choice of a name for it, and the one finally adopted was conferred upon it by members of an Italian opera cast, who included the island in a tour, and who applied to it the word referring to the quality of a high soprano voice. Another borrowed term used in the island was "chim-cham-bone," applied to the vegetable okra, for which no Spanish word was available; this also is an Italian contribution.

The machete, which I now show you, is the large knife which you see, and is used for working crops, building houses, and felling trees. In fact, it is a tool-of-all-work, as well as a weapon—the one in my hand is said to have killed three men. I once had a little carpentry job to do, and asked for what I considered the necessary tools, naming specifically a hammer, saw, hatchet, and screwdriver. The native to whom I addressed the request went out on the run and speedily reappeared with a machete, which he handed to me with the statement that "this will do the work of all of them."

The Island of Porto Rico is a little more than one hundred miles in length and about thirty-six miles in width. It has a population of nearly a million, of whom some 840,000 cannot read or write. Nearly 600,000 persons have never owned a single dollar's worth of property, and I might add that that includes clothing. I am, by nature, a laboring man and am in sympathy with the laboring classes. I should like to see every man own his home, completely paid for, but the poorest of our working classes have a cause for happiness by comparison with these natives. When I gaze upon these impoverished, downtrodden people, I rejoiced at being an American, even if it had meant only that I had something to wear. There were men and women in San Juan who never had enjoyed the experience of resting upon a bed with their heads on a pillow as we know it. Hundreds had never during their lives sat down to a table to eat their meals. A stroller along the streets at night might gaze down the hallways and corridors leading to the courtyards where the better classes kept their horses and chickens, and there see grownups and children lying asleep on the hard cement, like hogs on the floor of a pen.

And yet, when the sun rose on these same people next morning, they emerged to the streets wearing the most cheerful manner in the world, and moving with a dignity and pride which would have done credit to the Governor of the island. They were happy and contented, for they did not know of better things and did not know that they had anything better to look forward to or to pine after. Tuesday and Saturday of each week were known as "beggars' days," when the streets were lined from sunrise to sunset with the poor and afflicted asking alms. Among these were victims of elephantiasis and mild forms of leprosy, and on such days I took pains, if I could, not to be out upon the streets. All beggars, under the Spanish regime, were required to pay a license fee to practice their ancient profession, a practice which also is still prevalent in Spain and Mexico.

The contrast between the lower and upper classes is a great gulf—a mountain or an ocean which no man can cross. The better classes avail themselves of these poor people's labor for almost nothing by way of recompense. The pride of the pure-blooded Spaniards was intense, extending to a scorn of performing even such small tasks as carrying a little parcel through the streets, and they invariably called a peon for this and other trifling chores. My way is "when in Rome, do as the Romans do;" so, whenever I met a Spaniard, I tipped my hat, as he did, and I called a peon to carry my hand-grip as short a distance as across the street, so that I might retain the respect of the natives.

If you wish an introduction to a Spanish maiden, walk, smiling, down the street in front of her home. If she is looking, and she generally is, walk past again in the other

direction. Continue this procedure, and finally, if she is
satisfied with the results of her inspection, she, too, will
smile. Then you should return at the same hour punctually
for the next few days, and she will give you tokens of full
recognition and you will eventually be invited inside. The
rest of the courtship, as in any other environment the world
over, will be up to you.

In the seasons of the numerous fiestas and carnivals, ser-
pentinas (such as these I now throw out to you) are flung
from balconies and also fastened from house to house across
the streets, so that the city is invariably a beautiful and colorful sight. Papalites and cologned water shower down upon
the stroller from the houses. One young lady greeted me,
when I called upon her during a carnival, with a shower
of this scented water, and I, with due gallantry and knowledge—by that time—of the local customs, returned her
gesture by casting in her direction a handful of papalites.

No one ever lifts his voice to call to another. One merely hisses through his teeth, and all within range of the sound
look in the hisser's direction. The one at whom the sum-
mons is directed will then respond to a beckoning motion,
made with the front of the hand, and will come.

I was on my way to the steamship docks one day, when
I received one of the never-ending lessons in the finely
drawn distinctions that are attached to seemingly trifling
things by these folk. I saw passing in a carriage one of
my best señorita friends, who waved to me as we passed
each other. I stopped and waved back, using the back of
my hand in the gesture. She dropped her head and put
her handkerchief to her face, as if to indicate that something
had saddened her. I was worried, as I feared that, unaccustomed to some way of behavior, I might have done something improper. I afterward learned, however, that the
motion I had made conveyed the meaning farewell, and her

response was to evince sorrow at my supposed intention to depart. I should have waved with the palm of my hand.

All Americans there, at the same time I was, either married Spanish wives, or came to the United States for their spouses. A bachelor, who was a recent arrival on the island, heard me remark that something in the air of the place was driving everyone to drink or to matrimony. He scratched his head, stole a look at the girls then in his range of vision, and declared, "I guess I will take up drinking." Actually, that was what he did. But I believe that had he become acquainted with the families of the better class before he launched on his program to put this sudden resolution in effect, he would have remained a sober man and possibly might have had the happiness of becoming the husband of one of these many lovely girls.

It is a truthful saying that Porto Rico is the "land of mañana." That is the word—"tomorrow"—which they nearly always answer if any one wishes work done. They are believers in postponing until then almost any type of effort, and mañana in most cases never comes.

They are slow and will usually exert themselves only in order to attend a cockfight or participate in some other form of gaming.

In their cooking, they mix their meat, beans, and rice into one pot with a heavy flavoring of garlic—and the odor can only be described as horrible. I was unable to eat this mixture and many other native dishes, in common with most other Americans of the North, and often veered away from the windows to walk in the middle of the street, to escape the full force of the garlic aromas. Needless to say, the upper classes did not torture their food in this manner. Many of my meals, however, consisted of a raw egg broken into a cup of coffee. There were no refrigerated boats to bring perishable fruits or other foods to the island; so such things from outside sources were entirely lacking. While stopping at an "American" hotel, I once ordered what I had been assured in advance was "some fresh steak from the United States." I had taken several bites before I chanced to turn it over, and almost immediately thereafter I might have been seen hurrying from that place, never to return. A large stray cockroach was sticking to the underside of the meat.

High winds which are prevalent are useful in keeping most of the flies away, and the hurricane of 1899 had blown most of the birds away, or had killed them. Snakes are very scarce, but to make up for their absence, there are boundless numbers of tarantulas, centipedes, scorpions, chiggers and other pests. On some nights I was compelled to rise from my bed and shake out the fleas before I could continue my slumbers, which made me think of the ubiquitousness of the California flea.

Many times, as I sat at my desk in Porto Rico, I have looked up to find a large scorpion or tarantula interestedly returning my gaze. Large flying cockroaches occasionally whizzed through my rooms at night, as I have seen birds plummet across the sky above a Texas prairie. At one inland town's hotel, I was about to register, after making sure from the statement of the manager that he had a pest-free room. As I turned over the sheet, pen in hand, to inscribe my name, a tarantula of unusual size crawled upon the paper, as if to witness the signature. I told the hotel man, before turning to look for quarters elsewhere, that I felt in my bones that that big spider was checking the register in order to ascertain which room I was going to take, so that he might know where to find me.

Perhaps you have read that great heaps of human bones are customarily to be found in one corner of some Spanish burial tracts. These "graveyards" are owned by a company which rents the use of vaults by the year; and, if rentals are not received, the bones are "evicted" from the vault and piled with the other "defaulters," while the vault is rented to the next comer. The board of health now requires that the corpse be left in the vault for a period of five years, and that the bones be buried or burnt on removal.

A death among the natives is always followed by a ceremony which might be described as a "Spanish wake," where there is drinking but no drunkenness, and wherein there are funeral processions with well-defined conditions. For example, relatives and friends walk behind the hearse, if the family of the dead is able to afford one, with four persons attending the hearse holding dark ribbons that are attached to each of the vehicle's four corners. It is not customary for any woman to accompany the cortege unless the dead should be a child under six years old. I saw many of these funerals and followed several of them, and not once during my stay on the island did I see a woman in the procession.

The middle-class custom is to rent a bronze frame upon which the coffin, with the body inside, is laid; and the whole is covered with flowers and carried to the last resting place on the heads of four men whom draperies conceal from sight. It makes a beautiful and effective picture, this custom, which is known as "The Last Moving Train." Members of the lower classes ordinarily merely rent a coffin, which the father, in his poverty, often is compelled to carry himself, if the dead person is a child, upon his head. In this type of burial, the body, uncoffined, is gently laid to rest in the earth and the casket is returned to the undertaker for further renting. I was told that one particular coffin had conveyed many a dead body to the same burial tract, something difficult to believe.

The lower classes are poor, their poverty being so great as to be difficult to picture. Many live, without any toil whatsoever, on the wild-growing tropical fruits, and in one town of nearly ten thousand it was said that not fifty dollars in cash could have been raised among the entire population.

They are, however, very shrewd and extremely tricky, the two qualities counteracting each other somewhat.

The expressions most often heard on the streets and elsewhere are: "Mañana," "poco tiempo," and "no sabe," their respective English meanings being "tomorrow," "a little time," and "I don't understand." How often these words are used may best be shown by a little story involving the visit of a prominent United States government official who visited the island on some sort of investigative mission. I was observing the procession following the body in an unusually large funeral, at which this official was an onlooker. Noticing the size of the group, and observing that the natives all removed their hats as the cortege passed, as is customary in respect to the dead, this visitor conceived the idea that perhaps a great man—possibly an ex-governor—was being buried. In attempting to learn the identity of the body in whose honor the funeral was being held, he asked a peon standing near, receiving the almost universal answer, "No sabe." Believing the man had uttered a name, but not certain he had heard accurately, he repeated the question several times, getting the same reply each time. At last, in a gesture of impatience, he rubbed his head and exploded, "If they are actually burying this No Sabe today, I hope to the Lord they will bury that chap Mañana tomorrow."

I hope this has afforded you a faint conception of what you might have seen if you yourselves had been living in Porto Rico. Our Government has undertaken a great work in the island, and we have in this work a grave problem requiring the influence of every good Christian in this beautiful land of ours—a task we have assumed for the sake of humanity, to elevate these poor people to a high degree of civilization. It is fraught with danger unless all will lend helping hands, yet what a noble achievement it will be when it is finished! It can command the respect and admiration of

all the world—this work laid upon our nation by its martyred
Chief who is now with his Maker, but whose Christian life
and kindly deeds will make his name live forever in the
memory of his people. I refer to President William Mc-
Kinley.

I delivered this address in several states. At Evansville,
Indiana, a packed house, in which there was not a foot of
standing room, heard it, and afterward a man of fine appearance came up to me and, without introducing himself said,
"Dr. Cline, I came here tonight expecting to hear something
good. Your talk was even better than I had expected it to be
—among the best I ever have heard. I want to congratulate
you. I have traveled all over the world, and you told more
about a country in a few words than any speaker I have previously had the pleasure of hearing."

As I was leaving, later, a woman teacher of the public
schools there asked me if I knew the identity of the man who
had congratulated me thus. When I told her I did not, she
went on: "He is a famous lecturer, who has traveled the
world over. His compliments, when he tenders them, are
sincere, and you should take pride in the praise he accorded
your speech tonight."

Part of this lecture was obtained from clippings of daily
newspapers published in Porto Rico and the United States.
And while I was on the island my official Spanish translator
gave me information as to some of the customs and actions of
the natives.

CHAPTER VI

MARRIAGE AND WEATHER BUREAU WORK

My marriage to Miss Ula Jackson, the daughter of Judge James Jackson and Sarah Jackson, Texas pioneers and landowners, took place on December 18, 1901. Dr. Judson Palmer, secretary of the Young Men's Christian Association at Galveston, officiated. At the time, my wife was twenty-five years old and I was thirty-one.

After the ceremony we embarked upon a trip to Lookout Mountain, at Chattanooga, Tennessee, and other points of interest before returning to the Weather Bureau Station at Sandusky, Ohio. There we spent much of our time at a delightful summer resort near Johnson Island, where Confederate prisoners were detained during the war between the North and South, and, on many of his trips, the captain of the boat plying to the resort invited us to be his guests. Many pleasant afternoons and evenings we spent in this manner.

We were at Sandusky when President William McKinley was assassinated, the outstanding historical event of our stay there. I was later transferred to Evansville, Indiana, where we were fortunate enough to be associated with many friendly people prominently known in that city. My office was in the post-office building, and one day I was called by the postmaster into his office to meet Congressman James Hemenway, chairman of the Ways and Means Committee of the House and an outstanding figure of his day in Washington.

We had a chat together on that occasion and other meetings followed. During the second of these, Colonel Hemen-

Ula Jean Jackson at the age of 18

Joseph L. Cline, at the time of his marriage

way told me that he planned to attend the annual meeting
of the National Rivers and Harbors Convention at Cincin-
nati. He further explained that he had accepted an invitation to make a speech there and invited me to help him by
supplying some information on meteorology, adding that he
had been informed that I had made an extensive study of the
Ohio and its tributaries.

I presented him with a list of the figures I had compiled,
assuring him that they had been checked and found to be
completely accurate. He utilized most of my data, making
some changes in the verbiage so that the original source
could not be detected, and his address was so successful that
the Associated Press dispatches paid him high compliments
upon it. He afterward wrote me a personal letter of thanks
and said he stood ready at any time to repay the favor.

Before we had been there long, we became deeply attached to Evansville and to many of its residents; but we
both wanted to return to Texas, where we had interests in
real estate and where my wife's family made their home. I
wrote, therefore, a special letter to the Chief of the Weather
Bureau at Washington, stating my reasons for desiring to
make a change, and in a short time received the response
that I should be relieved as soon as a replacement at Evansville could be found for me. The letter continued that my
orders of transfer would assign me to Corpus Christi, Texas,
where I would assume charge of the Bureau located there.

In a few days the promised order arrived, and I released to the local newspapers the news of my forthcoming
departure. Next day I was again asked to come to the postmaster's office, where Colonel Hemenway was waiting to see
me. There, Colonel Hemenway handed me a telegram he
had received from the Evansville *Evening Journal,* one of
Indiana's most highly regarded papers, reading as follows:

"Colonel Hemenway, Chairman Ways and Means
Committee,
Washington, D. C.

Doctor Joseph Cline in charge of Weather Bureau
here has been ordered away. He is the best weather
man we have ever had. We urgently request you to
stop transfer.

(Signed) Manager The Evening Journal,
Evansville, Indiana."

Colonel Hemenway commented that he had entrained at
Washington and traveled all night to see me, before acting
on the transfer order. His committee, he went on, was
charged with responsibility of approving the annual appropriation of the Department of Agriculture, which included the
Weather Bureau, and he added that he was empowered, as
chairman of the Ways and Means Committee, to hold up the
appropriation until the Chief of the Weather Bureau awarded me promotion. This, he said, he would be glad to do if
I would consent to remain in Evansville.

I thanked him warmly, but I explained my reasons for requesting the move. My wife, I said, desired to be closer to
her own people, and we were losers in a monetary way by
being unable from such a distance to protect our Texas interests. He was prompt in saying that he understood fully
my position in the matter, and again urged me to call upon
him whenever he could serve me in the future.

We left Evansville and its congenial people in the year
1903, with considerable regret. However, we found our new
home, Corpus Christi, also a well-situated and pleasant place
in which to live, and we soon made many good friends there,
as well. It had enjoyed a boom of considerable proportion

previously, and a reaction of depression had ensued, with most of the Corpus Christi homes in need of repairs and renovation.

When we had become well settled there, we paid a visit to Chambers County, where we owned interests in grazing property and some irrigated rice acreage. The summer had been dry, and the Trinity River had fallen so low as to become a mere thread of water running between parched banks. At Anahuac, Texas, where the irrigation pump was situated, the pumping plant's owner told me he had been compelled to pump salt water over the rice fields, and gloomily predicted that if conditions remained as they were, the land would be ruined within a five-year period. After I had had opportunity to inspect the pump, I inquired why no rock dykes or jetties had been constructed from the west side of Anahuac Bay, at a point above the pump, down to it at an angle of about forty-five degrees. This, I pointed out, would convey to the pump all the water coming down the Trinity, while forcing the salt water back into the lower bay. Admitting the need for such construction, he answered that no money was available for such jetties.

I made a quick pencil sketch of the point at which the Trinity entered the bay, together with details showing the location of the pump. I told the owner that I possessed a friend in Congress who would, I felt certain, arrange for the needed funds. That night I mailed the sketches, together with a letter, to Colonel Hemenway, informing him fully of the predicament with which we were faced. In the letter, I told him my wife and I were interested in the rice land that was under irrigation there, and urged him to take such action as might be required to protect this land from damage by salt water.

In less than ten days the reply came back, informing me that he had arranged with the United States Engineer at

Galveston to start survey for a rock jetty in Anahuac Bay within the next few days, and he added, "As soon as we receive an estimate of the cost we will rush the necessary appropriation for speediest possible completion of the job." It was but a short time after that the rock jetty was built at a cost which I learned was about $25,000. Today, more than twenty-five years later, the irrigation plant at Anahuac is still pumping the water from the river with good results over the rice fields there. Needless to say, I have always felt that many more men like Colonel Hemenway could be sent with advantage to the halls of Congress.

On returning to Corpus Christi, I embarked upon the consistent purchase of real estate. On one occasion I encountered in the courthouse, Eli Merriman, editor of the Corpus Christi *Caller*. I was in the act of filing a deed to some lots, and he remarked that it was the first such instrument filed there in five years. Next day, an article was published in his newspaper, calling attention to the fact that "Dr. Joseph L. Cline of the U. S. Weather Bureau is buying real estate in this city." The item further stated that the fact proved my faith in such real estate's prospects of coming again into its own, upon completion of the new railroad which would extend from Houston, through Corpus Christi, into Brownsville.

A short time after publication of this article, I began to get letters. They poured in from dwellers in the Philippine Islands, from residents of the Hawaiian Islands, and from persons living elsewhere abroad, as well as from others making their homes in various parts of the United States. Most of the writers, it seemed, had bought lots there during the previous boom in Corpus Christi, and now wished to sell their properties. Their lot, ran the characteristic tenor of these communications, was Number So-and-So, and would I look at the tract and make an offer based upon my judgment of its worth? I made many such offers and in all cases received the owners' acceptances by mail, in which also they requested deeds, the kind I wished them to execute. When I had purchased all the lots that I found desirable, I turned to the construction of houses on these sites, and these I sold on the installment plan of payment. The Houston-to-Brownsville rail line had meanwhile reached completion, and real estate values had made the advance that I had foreseen. The public exaggerated, in their talk of these deals, the amount of profit I derived, but I will admit to making some money; and I believe it can be said that I was instrumental in originating in Corpus Christi the boom that followed the building of the railroad, and that has continued up to the present time.

I was frequently called upon, while I was a resident there, for public appearances of one sort or another, in line with my knowledge and my official position. I was for several years an instructor in the high school, teaching meteorology to senior and sub-senior classes, and I was a special lecturer in meteorology and kindred subjects at the Texas State Normal Institute, which was held for two years at Corpus Christi for an area comprising a large section of the state. In my teaching, I frequently asked questions of a technical nature, inviting replies that would indicate the amount of knowledge possessed by the more than four hundred teachers in attendance upon the Institute, who were there studying for their certificates to teach in the state's public schools. One of these involved a cup of water which had been heated to near the boiling point, which I displayed to the audience along with a standard Weather Bureau mercurial thermometer. What, I asked, would be the first change that would take place when I should immerse the bulb end of the thermometer in the water?

Nearly all the teachers raised their hands for a chance to

answer, and their answers were all the same. The mercury, according to their unanimous verdict, would rise in the bulb. Informing them that this was in error, I inquired whether anyone present could give me the correct response. Professor Menger, head of the Institute and superintendent of the city's high school, correctly stated that under such conditions the glass would expand, so that the mercury would drop slightly, after which it would rise nearly to the temperature of the water.

I was an appointed member of the committee to welcome President Taft on the occasion of the latter's official visit to Southwest Texas. The committee met his boat in the Gulf and extended him a cordial invitation to come ashore for a stopover, an invitation which he accepted. He also spent a few days with his brother at the Taft Ranch, in San Patricio County.

I was honored with the selection to be principal speaker at the Chamber of Commerce celebration of Lincoln's Birthday. In my remarks on this occasion I stated what has always been a conviction of mine: That the South would have gained by a prolongation of the President's life. I said that I felt, if he had lived, he might have assembled the colored population in a country of their own, with self-rule under the United States Government—a sort of protectorate. The colored and the white races would each have been better off under such conditions, I told them, and the danger of race riots or antagonisms would have been virtually eliminated. When I had concluded this talk, many leading citizens came from the audience to congratulate me, some saying that I had placed an original and, to them, unheard-of construction upon Mr. Lincoln's possible intentions, but that they believed it was the correct view.

At the time, Corpus Christi was without a sewerage system, and, when I built my own home, I installed two septic tanks, one to serve my own residence and the other for the use of the building in which the Weather Bureau offices were located.

Septic tanks are capable of being used for a long time. When well constructed, in sandy subsoil, they will not be filled for about twenty years, as only one ounce of solid matter forms each day through use by eleven persons, and some of this, even, passes off with water through the sand.

However, there was a move on foot to build a municipal sewage-disposal system on the low bottom land of the Nueces River, and city health officers and members of the city commission had already met in consideration of such a project. The plan was that the proposed plant be constructed at a point from which the sewage flow-off would pass into the river above a large oyster bed; and no provision had been made for a charcoal filter bed to purify the waste. The oyster bed was the only one near Corpus Christi, and one of the councilmen, an attorney, had urged me to appear before the council meeting at which final decision was to be made—initial approval having already been voted—and to warn the city fathers against the danger that would result from the installation of an open and unprotected sewerage plant.

I came before the council and told them the story of an historic episode that took place once in England. A Privy Council, which corresponds to the city council in our cities, had installed a disposal plant similar in principle to the one contemplated in Corpus Christi. One of the Privy Council members was owner of a large oyster bed at a point just below the English disposal plant, from which a charcoal filter bed had been omitted. I went on to describe how, a few weeks after the building of the plant, some oysters from the bed below were served at an elaborate entertainment, and about thirty guests contracted typhoid fever shortly afterward. Health officers of that day traced the source of the fever to the oyster bed, condemned it, and forbade its use. The owner brought suit against the Privy Council, seeking damages; and, though the council's contention, that he had voted as a member to install the sewerage plant, was sustained in a lower court, the upper court awarded damages to him on appeal on the ground that his vote alone would have been insufficient to authorize the installation. The higher court also pointed out that "even though the owner of the bed be entitled to damages, he and the entire Privy Council are subject to criminal prosecution for contaminating the oysters with typhoid germs, resulting in many deaths caused by eating of the oysters."

This talk apparently had its effect, for the council altered its plans and included in the project a large charcoal bed for filtration purposes. Since its construction, not to this day has there been any report of typhoid germs in that section of Texas. The fact is now well known that water passing over several acres of charcoal flows off as clear and as pure as— or even purer than—the drinking water used in many parts of the country.

The offer to make me mayor of the city took place when one day I was engaged in inspection of some residences I was building in the suburbs, and I learned of it in a chance meeting with a friend of mine who was a large-scale contractor and house mover. He told me that a move was afoot to elect me as mayor, adding that "we wish you would accept, as we feel certain that you are the man to help us in building a great city here. The committee is planning to call upon you before the day is over. You must promise to aid us by standing for the office."

When the committee arrived, however, I thanked them for the honor they wished to accord me, but told them, much as I appreciated their proposal, I could not afford to leave my job with the Government for that purpose.

At Corpus Christi I went through my second experience with the Gulf storms. A pretty severe hurricane formed, and warnings were displayed up and down the Texas Coast. Conditions pointed to the probability that the blow would strike southeast of the city, and I placed a telephone call to Mayor Cotter, of Tarpon, a small Texas city of about five hundred population on a little island south of Port Aransas. My advice to him, upon getting the connection, was to obtain a boat and to take the people off the island to the mainland. I also sent officers to patrol the beach at Corpus Christi and to warn those living in the lowlands to close up their homes and spend the night in the high bluffs sector of the town. I learned afterward that Mayor Cotter acted upon my advice, and that virtually all of the lowland dwellers did likewise. The low-lying homes were flooded, and Tarpon was in effect washed completely away—all houses damaged—but not a single life was lost, so far as my reports showed. The city had another such hurricane shortly after I received my transfer to another station, resulting in several hundred deaths by drowning and in considerable property damage around the Bay. Eli Merriman, Mr. Bigo, and other residents of Corpus Christi who afterward visited me stated with conviction that, if I had remained there, no lives need have been lost had I proceeded with my warnings as before.

My vegetables, which I cultivated myself on a vacant lot adjoining my house in Corpus Christi were widely known in a time when the winter vegetable was a rarity. Truck peddlers gathered those which I did not use for my family's needs, and paid over to me sufficient sums from their sale to pay all of my rent during the winter that my permanent home was under construction. In addition, my garden was made a point of interest to real estate "prospectors" from the North, brought to the city by realty salesmen, who never failed to give the visitors a look at the fine crop of winter vegetables grown on the Texas coast.

Events leading up to my departure from Corpus Christi began with a special message received one day from Prof. Moore, the Bureau Chief, asking me to inform him whether or not I should like an appointment as Section Director for South Carolina, with Columbia, S. C., as Section Center. After talking the matter over with my wife, I informed the Chief that I should prefer assignment to be in charge of the proposed Weather Bureau office at Dallas, Texas, should a station be established there. Before relating the details of my transfer there, however, I will set down some facts about my record that probably led to my obtaining the post of my choice so easily.

During my stay at Corpus Christi, the Chief required all officials in charge of stations to make a special forecast for their home area and for one outer station, as a test of forecasting ability. Only those forecasts involving precipitation and temperature changes were verified, and the records of these were compared with the "standard forecasts," which were those issued at Forecast Division, in Washington, or at district forecast centers.

My first outer station for these tests was Fort Smith, Arkansas, from which I received not a single report to give me a line on the weather conditions there, so I was forced to base my forecasts for this point on conditions noted at Little Rock, Ark., and at Oklahoma City, Okla. Yet, when the results had been verified and forwarded to me, I found that I was making a better record in forecasting Fort Smith weather than was the official in charge there, or than the district forecaster himself was able to compile. When Oklahoma City was later given me as the outer station, I was able to achieve the same record there; and it was the same story at Amarillo, Texas. During one month's time, Amarillo had only one rain, which I predicted correctly and which the district forecaster and official in charge failed to foresee. And, for that month, my feat gave me a rating of fifty per cent over the record of the Standard Forecast, to my justifiable pride.

Woodrow Wilson, soon after his election to the Presidency, named a special committee comprising the Assistant Secretary of Agriculture, of whose department the Weather Bureau was a part; Dr. Charles F. Marvin, Chief of the Instrument Division, who was later Chief of the Weather Bureau; and, as a third member, an unidentified person. This committee was charged with investigating the Bureau for the President.

In the process, civil service rules were suspended, and employees were instructed to request promotions, if they believed they were justified on merit in so doing, and to state the reasons for their belief that they might be entitled to advancement. My wife, who was present when I received the letter containing these instructions, remarked, "You are certainly going to ask for the promotion, aren't you?" I tried to tell her that it was only part of a political move to remove the Chief of the Bureau, but she persisted so emphatically in the opinion that I should make the request that I finally told her we would let chance decide, and I flipped a half dollar. She called, "Heads," and won; accordingly, I wrote my application, giving the following reasons:

"During the past nine years," I wrote, "I have taken two observations daily and prepared all station meteorological forms as Officer in Charge at Corpus Christi, Texas. At all times I have had as assistant only a messenger boy—often a new and untrained boy. The checking of forms and of work of the Station by Central Office employees has resulted in my being charged with only one error during the nine-year period to which I refer; I enclose the 'error letters' to confirm this statement. (I later learned this was a record for the Bureau.)

"I also enclose three letters declaring that reports of Weather Bureau inspectors have found the station 'in excellent condition.'

"I tender further letters as evidence that, for the past two years, my daily forecasts have bettered Standard Forecasts at both my home station and the outer station assigned me. During one of these years, only five other employees of the Bureau achieved that record; and, during the other year, only eleven others equaled it.

"I have summarized all records covering each year since this Station was established, up to now."

Apparently my Washington record also spoke strongly in my behalf, indicating, as it must have, the results of my work in saving crops and property, coupled with expressions of appreciation by the Corpus Christi public. And among the letters I enclosed in my letter of request was evidence that many Officials in Charge had had their authority to make local forecasts for the stations suspended, notwithstanding the fact that their salaries were in excess of my own.

I received my promotion. Bureau records show that the President's committee ordered that I be granted advancement, while the same body demoted fifty or more of the Bureau's higher officials.

My orders to report to Dallas and there establish a regular Weather Bureau Station were received shortly after this bit of good fortune for me. Dallas had up to that time maintained only a co-operative station, under supervision of Mr. G. A. Eisenlohr, one of the leading citizens of Dallas.

In the month of July, 1913, I arrived in Dallas, the city which from that time on was destined to be my home, and established that city's first regular Weather Bureau office in the Dallas Cotton Exchange Building on Akard Street, now known as the Construction Building. (The Bureau was afterward moved to the new Cotton Exchange Building, on St. Paul Street, where it remained until it was consolidated with the Love Field Airway Service; after that, the general weather service was lost to the public because of the fact that the Airway Service was given preference in the consolidation.) Airway Service at Love Field was under my supervision during a period of several years, and I was successful in obtaining for Love Field the first Airway Forecast Section Center in the Southwest. This center was afterwards moved to Fort Worth, Texas, where it is still situated, and where all state airway forecasts for Texas and adjacent states are issued. Dallas is among the cities depending upon this forecast, along with other airports in the Fort Worth district. General weather forecasts for Louisiana, Arkansas, and Texas east of the hundredth meridian, which includes Dallas and its vicinity, are issued daily at the District Forecast Center at New Orleans, Louisiana, and forwarded to Dallas and the other points covered for release there.

I bought a home not long after my transfer to Dallas— a house on East Eighth Street—and other pieces of property in the Oak Cliff section of the city. The City of Dallas paved East Eighth, omitting, however, to pave that portion of the street leading to Oak Cliff Cemetery, although this was the only major highway leading east out of Oak Cliff.

At a meeting of the Oak Cliff Chamber of Commerce, I raised my voice against this omission. I said that it was a reflection on the civic pride of Oak Cliff and of Dallas as a whole, to permit that portion of the street adjacent to the cemetery to continue unpaved, leaving, as it did, an ugly, block-long gap, which was almost impassable in muddy weather.

The City Commissioners had admitted that this condition was regrettable, but explained that lack of funds had made paving impracticable for the cemetery side of the highway, and pointed out further that attempts by various groups, including a committee of women whose loved ones were buried in the cemetery, to raise sums for defraying the costs of this paving project had been unsuccessful. These facts were called to my attention by some of the leading members of the Oak Cliff Chamber after I had had my say, and several of them said that obtaining the needed funds was an impossible task. I answered that I did not believe it impossible, and the meeting finally made a concession: I was authorized to have the thoroughfare paved, provided it was not paved at the Chamber's expense.

Mr. Milton H. McConnell, manager of the Chamber for a period of five years, joined his signature to mine at the close of a letter issued at my own expense, which was mailed to each owner of a lot in the cemetery. The letter elicited mostly varying forms of indifference. Then, although I myself was not a lot owner, I induced Mr. Johnson, a resident of Oak Cliff who had relatives buried there, to aid me in raising funds, and he entered into this project with enthusiasm. Together we made nightly calls upon various lot-owners, some of whom were difficult and in one case, even profane, at the start of these conferences. When we had fully explained our plan, however, we were almost invariably successful, and the man who had cursed the idea in the beginning tendered us five dollars for the fund after we had assured him that all of the money would go to paving and improving the area, adding, "I hope that you will be able to get the work done."

After several weeks of such visits, we had raised an amount adequate to the paving of the entire block, and to the laying of a sidewalk, in addition to the installing of curb and gutter. When all subscriptions were in, we even found that we had sufficient sums over and above the cost of improvements previously mentioned, to gravel the streets running through the cemetery. We had inserted an advertisement in the daily newspapers, asking that no more contributions be made, and yet we still had enough left over to purchase a number of lots in Laurel Land Memorial Park, then a new cemetery on South Beckley, operated under the same management as the old Oak Cliff Cemetery.

These lots were purchased and placed in the hands of the Oak Cliff Chamber of Commerce, with the stipulation that anyone unable to purchase a lot might be given burial privileges in one of these. I have been told that the new cemetery's management set aside some five hundred lots, by the use of which, persons unable to furnish burial expenses for their dead need not resort to paupers' graves. The total cost was placed at about three thousand dollars, but the end result was worth it—eliminating the need for any citizen of Dallas to be buried in the old paupers' cemetery along the banks of the Trinity southeast of the city.

This effort of mine recently received the following recognition, in a statement written by Mr. Milton McConnell recalling certain parts of my career:

"Dr. Joseph L. Cline, a former director of the Oak Cliff Chamber of Commerce, never undertook an assignment that he did not carry through to fruition. One instance was the paving of the old Oak Cliff Cemetery and the purchase of burial ground for those who might be unable to purchase cemetery lots. Dr. Cline undertook this job when many considered it time wasted in trying to put the project over. Today, largely due to his efforts, the Oak Cliff Cemetery is paved after years of neglect. Dr. Cline never shirked in putting in hours of labor for his community, or in opening his own pocketbook to aid any cause that was for the benefit of Oak Cliff or even Dallas proper."

Before my coming to Dallas, and after, I was in considerable demand as speaker before luncheon clubs and other meetings, on meteorological and kindred subjects. During one address delivered to the Texas Academy of Science, in annual session at the Adolphus Hotel, I was asked by Dr. Foscue, of Southern Methodist University, for my opinion on the "dry method" of farming then being talked about in Kansas. I told the group that it was a good method, as I had enjoyed the opportunity of seeing when it was practiced by my father on his farm when I was a small boy, away back in 1880, under the name, at that time, of "intensified cultivation." I explained that my father always had us plow corn immediately after every rain, at the earliest moment the soil had become sufficiently dry for cultivation. Using this method, we never had a corn failure during the twenty years I spent on the farm.

I was still a newcomer to Dallas when I was invited to speak before the Rotary Club, one of the leading civic groups, and my speech closed with the following story of drouths and weather conditions:

When I lived in the northern part of the country, I grew to be so interested in the subject of Texas and its weather that whenever I met a Texan, I asked him how he liked the climate of that state. One recently returned visitor to Texas answered this question by saying that he "would not live there. When I visited there in July and August, there was not one green leaf on the trees or a single green grass-blade on the prairies." (This was evidently in southwest Texas, where I have observed such conditions during the dry fall periods.)

Much later, I met a wealthy man who had recently concluded a visit to Texas during the fall and winter months, and who had obviously enjoyed one of the warm winters on the Texas Coast. (I have spent such winters, without a single frost, in that region myself.) To my question, he responded that "it is the garden spot of the world! During my stay there, roses, oleanders and other flowers were blooming in the out-of-doors; vegetables were growing under cultivation in profusion; and ripe strawberries were being picked and marketed in large quantities. I have returned here, where we have nothing growing during the winter seasons, in order to sell all my property here before returning to Texas to spend the rest of my days on earth. While in Texas, I dreamed that I had died and was about to enter Heaven; answering my knock on the Pearly Gates, St. Peter said 'Who art thou?' On hearing my name (the visitor went on) he bade me enter and asked me whence I had come. I answered, 'From Texas' and he motioned me in a certain direction. Crossing a line which had been drawn, I was seized and chained securely, so that it was impossible to move far in any direction. Later, as St. Peter passed by I called to ask him why I, and others. were chained when those on the other side of the line were permitted to roam at will along the Golden Streets. He answered, 'Young man! Didn't you say you came from Texas? Then don't you know that, in order to keep Texans here in Heaven from returning to that magnificent and glorious place, we are compelled to chain them?' "

It fell to my lot to submit the first scheme ever drawn up for forecasting floods in the Trinity River, which flows through Fort Worth and Dallas, and south to the Gulf. A letter from the Chief informed me that the entire program of river work in Texas was being revised. and that, if I could handle it, the Trinity would be assigned to me instead of to the Houston station. I was directed to furnish a scheme for forecasting the floods, and the plan, which was approved by the Official in Charge of the River and Flood Division at Washington, authorized me to issue river and flood warnings for the river's upper area.

The warnings, many of which I subsequently issued under this authorization, proved to be exceptionally accurate, causing my record in river forecasting to speak for itself. As an example of the confidence my consistent success in this respect achieved, I called the sheriff, Mr. Brandenburg, during the second largest flood that has ever occurred at Dallas, requesting him to get residents of West Dallas out of danger in the river bottom-lands, and Mr. Brandenburg told me a few days later, of an incident in which one man—assistant engineer of the Oriental Hotel—had refused to heed my warning and leave the perilous area. This man, according to the story told to me, asserted that he had "just talked to Dr. Cline," and that I had told him the river's further rise would not be more than a foot. I had never, this man stubbornly insisted, missed my mark on a forecast made in Dallas, and he was firm in his intention to stand fast now on the strength of my prophecy.

Mr. Brandenburg said the engineer's house was flooded and his furniture hoisted upon tables, along with the other household goods, but that the owner grimly remained, although he sent his family to dry land in a boat. Incidentally, the man in question was among the closest of all followers of my forecasts, calling me daily during expected flood periods in order to obtain information which he might pass on in warning persons living in the lowlands.

"That man certainly exhibited the utmost confidence in you, Dr. Cline," Mr. Brandenburg said at the conclusion of this narrative. "With over two feet of water throughout his home, and the river still rising—with all his possessions piled on the tops of tables—he took your statement, as to the final limits to which the flood would go, as his Gospel, and stayed to guard his property. Under these conditions, I'm afraid that I would have left my home to its fate."

Under Governor James E. Ferguson, a fifty-member committee of prominent and influential Texans was appointed, composed of men interested in foresty work in the state, to work out a program for improving and saving the Texas forests. Among the members were Mr. Goodrich Jones, Mr. R. A. Gilliam and myself. We were instructed to confer, and to work out and recommend a special bill for presentation to the State Legislature, looking to the establishment of a Texas State Forestry Association.

The committee met in Dallas and proposed an act which was passed by the Legislature, as a result of which, among other moves, may be noted the improved status of forests in Texas today. For this improvement, credit is due to the foresight of the then Governor and Legislature of the state. The Texas Forestry Association, after initiating passage of the law in question, continued to be active, with Mr. Goodrich Jones, of Temple, Texas, as president. At the time of this writing, Mr. Jones is president emeritus. Mr. R. A. Gilliam, former city forester at Dallas, also served a term as head of the organization. It has been truthfully said that Texas is fortunate in having men who are forward-looking and who are dynamic in achievements which aim at benefiting the coming generations.

On instructions from Washington, where the Chief of the Weather Bureau had received a request from Governor Pat Neff to send a special representative, I attended at Austin, the state capital, a meeting, called by the Governor, of engineers and other prominent Texans for the purpose of working out a proposed law to establish a "State Reclamation Service and Flood Control." In a brief talk, I assured the assemblage that the Chief of the Weather Bureau was much interested in the project and I informed the gathering that all records of the Bureau were at their disposal. I received, in return, the personal thanks of the Governor, to be conveyed

to the Chief, for the co-operation thus offered. The proposed
service was ultimately put into effect.

The program of establishing Federal Business Associa-
tions was inaugurated while I was stationed in Dallas. The
Federal Government, by Act of Congress, set up the position of co-ordinator, who was placed at the head of government activities. Positions of area co-ordinators, with officials
in charge, also were established. Under the area co-ordinator
in charge of Texas and other Southwestern states, with headquarters at Fort Sam Houston, San Antonio, Texas, was the
Dallas Federal Business Association for an area including
Northeast Texas, extending from the Red River to south of
Mexia, and lying east of Fort Worth.

It was while I was president of the Dallas Federal Business Association that Congressman Fish, of New York,
authorized a resolution which was passed by Congress, requiring the area co-ordinator to investigate and submit a full
report on activities of Communism. As head of the Dallas
area, it fell to me to be responsible for submission of such a
report.

The Communists, or Socialists, were holding public meetings about that time, with a view to swelling membership
lists, and it came to my attention that such a meeting was to
be held publicly at Fair Park, in Dallas, on a designated
evening.

In accordance with my instructions, I set about obtaining
information concerning this meeting for my report. I approached the city police department, the sheriff's office and
the United States marshal in turn, with the request that
some one appointed by each, attend the meeting and furnish
me with details for a special report to the Federal Government. I was told at each of these offices that the personnel
were too busy to comply with my request. As it was necessary that this information be obtained, I attended myself,

accompanied by my first assistant, Mr. William B. Shope. As a result, the following report was forwarded to the area co-ordinator at Fort Sam Houston:

"This is to advise that Communism has spread and that there are organizers now forming a council in Dallas.

"At 10 A. M., on Friday, February 20, 1931, a man known as Commodore Cody held a public demonstration at Fair Park here, and made a Communistic talk, criticizing the Government and personally mentioning the President, by name, in language unbecoming to an American citizen. There were several hundred people at the meeting, Negroes, Mexicans and white people, who were mostly out of work.

"At the close of the lecture, the speaker passed out cards headed: Application for Membership Unemployed Council. After obtaining about seventy-five signatures, the speaker said he had no more application cards but that he had sent for another supply. The meeting elected a secretary and other officers, making for a complete organization. Three delegates were elected to attend a public demonstration at the Capitol at Austin on February 25.

"In his talk, Cody advocated impossible things, too numerous to mention. He read an especially prepared paper, written by men who were evidently higher up in the Order, and stated that they also stood for a program of giving each unemployed man fifteen dollars weekly, plus two dollars additional for each other member of the family. Many other things were advocated which were especially alluring to persons out of employment.

"Cody also stated that there was to be a public demonstration held on February 25, throughout the United States and in every other nation, including Russia.

"Copy of application for membership card and newspapers, which has been distributed in Dallas, is enclosed. Those who signed application for membership were furnished literature at little or no cost.

"Respectfully submitted by the Committee on Communism,

Joseph L. Cline, Chairman."

As we were returning to the office, Mr. Shope asked me my opinion of the meeting. I answered that if all the promises made by the speaker could be permanently fulfilled by the Government, I would tell those in charge of such a program to take my property and avoid useless delay; but I added that, in my opinion, such an activity would be too costly to keep in force for many years. I must now add, however, that the New Deal has apparently covered several of the proposals which the speaker at that meeting advocated.

About two weeks after the occasion of which I have just written, an interesting event took place. A lone Texas Ranger entered my office. I was acquainted with him, and invited him to sit down until I could finish telephoning weather forecasts to the newspapers and to the Associated Press and International News Service. When I had completed this routine, and had turned back to my visitor, he opened his coat to display his Ranger badge. I assured him that I had already recognized him as a State Ranger from a previous contact with him in South Texas, and inquired the purpose of his visit.

He told me, then, that in some localities of Texas wherein Communistic meetings had been held, men had been taken out and whipped, and finally ordered to leave the country. Then he asked me if I knew the identity of those involved in perpetrating any of these whippings.

Smiling at the absurdity of this question, I asked him, in turn, why he had not gone to the police in the cities where the floggings had occurred.

He answered: "I have been to them. They tell me that they do not know the identity of the guilty persons."

"Then why have you come to see me?" I inquired.

"Because I know that you have made a report about Communism, and believed that you might have other information on the subject," he responded.

I questioned him as to the source of his knowledge about the report, and he gave me the following details:

A copy of my report (he said) was sent to the Governor of Texas and to the Adjutant General. The delegates to whom the report had referred began arriving in Austin some five days before the appointed meeting day, and officers had been stationed along all highways leading into the capital for the purpose of preventing a congested situation by warning visitors away from the city. But for my report, he added, Austin would have "experienced one of the worst traffic jams in its history."

"Even as it was," he said, "movement throughout the city was excessively difficult for several days."

After he had finally been convinced that I knew nothing of the floggings, he asked for Mr. Shope and put the same question to him, much to the latter's amusement also at this far-fetched line of investigation. The Ranger, finally explaining that he had been directed by the Governor to investigate and to make a report on the matter, took his leave.

It has always seemed strange to me that confusion has existed in some minds as to the meaning of a forecast on the weather, when the prediction was clearly stated. When I was in charge of the Dallas Bureau, with years of experience in forecasting and one of the top records in the land to my official credit, I would occasionally be encountered with the suggestion that I had made a particular forecast, when actually an entirely different type of weather had been prophesied. From this inaccurate belief, and from chance conversation resulting from it, circulation would from time to time be given to the public that I had missed my forecast, even though the original forecast had been confirmed by developments to the last detail.

This, to me, peculiar circumstance played a part on one occasion in a court proceeding, in which was involved testimony as to the nature of the weather on a particular day. That was one time when my rebuttal of the injustice of the "wrong forecast" accusation went into the judicial records, for I induced the judge to send for the official report of that occasion, as filed in my office, and thus obtained court recognition that the forecast I had issued was correct.

I do not feel that I am unduly vain about my accuracy in forecasting; but that was my business and, without excessive pride, I can say that on the overwhelming majority of occasions I predicted the weather during the periods of the forecasts with complete accuracy. And, as to those who have doubtless circulated false reports concerning my work and me, I can only say, without rancor, that they were "probably full of the truth, as they never let any of it out."

As an example, a resident of one city in which I was stationed at the time was a visitor at the office of the Weather Bureau in Chicago, where he made the statement to the official in charge that I had made the sum of fifty thousand dollars. The news moved along, finally reaching the Chief of the Weather Bureau, at Washington, who promptly sent an inspector to look into what I was doing.

The inspector's report on the station termed it "in excellent condition"—the first time, I have been told by men long in the service, that this phrase was ever used by that inspector in such a report.

Nevertheless, a second inspector followed the first within a short time. His report also used the words "in excellent condition." Yet a third inspector followed the second in no great time thereafter. This man took up a line of questioning which was altogether irrelevant, such as the subjects of politics and religion, which may not legitimately be considered as related to appointments in the United States service. Among other things, he asked me if I ever went to church.

Without a smile, I answered:

"I have only attended church one time since the Galveston Hurricane. You will recall that in Galveston scarcely a church was left standing. On the other hand, not a saloon was damaged. One Sunday, while out for a walk, I stepped into what I took to be a saloon. It turned out to be a church, so, out of respect to the congregation, I remained until the services were over."

The inspector's face reddened perceptibly, in the knowledge that he had asked an improper question. Mumbling that he knew that I never drank, he terminated the interview right there, and departed—and for a third time in rapid succession my station got the report: "In excellent condition."

One of the big football "bowl games," the Dallas annual Cotton Bowl Classic, may be cited to illustrate how vital a part weather forecasts can play in an epic business or civic event. In 1938, Mr. Curtis Sanford was manager of the second New Year's game billed under this title, in which Rice Institute was to play the University of Colorado.

The outlook for the event was less than favorable. There had been rain every day and night during the final week of December. Five days before the day of the game, a representative of the Associated Press telephoned me from Mr. Sanford's office in the Adolphus Hotel to put to me what was, from the viewpoint of the game's sponsors, a very vital question.

"I am calling," the press man said, "because there is a great deal of worry here over the constant rains. Mr. Sanford has it in mind to spend some thirty thousand dollars in advertising the event, in the hope of bringing here the largest number of visitors ever assembling in Dallas. I am aware that you are not permitted to forecast the weather so far in advance as New Year's Day, but I should like to have your opinion as to whether the indications, meteorologically speaking, would seem to justify the expenditure of such a large amount."

I told him that it would be utterly impossible to form an accurate opinion so many days ahead, but invited him to remain on the line long enough to enable me to consult the morning weather map. After a few moments of concentrated study of this document, I returned to the telephone and gave as my opinion that the rain would, according to indications, continue for a few additional days. I further said, however, that, if weather conditions moved across the country according to the track they were taking at that time, the rain should cease in time for the game.

"What would your advice be, then?" he asked.

"I would spend the money for the advertising and take out some rain insurance for protection," I answered. He thanked me and said that they would follow this course.

It kept on raining steadily, and, on the night before the game, the same Associated Press representative called me again from Mr. Sanford's office, informing me that they had just received the District Forecast Center report from New Orleans predicting rain for that night and the next day.

"I hesitated to call you at home," he said, "but, since it is still raining here in Dallas, Mr. Sanford is anxious for your opinion about the possibility that the game will be spoiled by more rainfall tomorrow."

"My own forecast for Dallas and its vicinity, issued this morning, was for rain tonight, ceasing in time for the football game tomorrow, as you doubtless noted," I answered.

"Despite the fact that the state forecast predicts rain to-morrow, I continue to be of the opinion that we shall have a good day."

This opinion was confirmed when the rain stopped that night and the sky cleared on the following morning, making the weather for the Cotton Bowl all that could be desired.

The football spectacle, on which so much depended and which hinged in such large part on the condition of the weather on that particular New Year's day, was a complete success, with such a vast crowd that many were unable to jam their way into the Bowl and were forced to return home disappointed. The event was termed, by many, one of the outstanding games of its kind ever staged, and there was a general call for the annual contest, which was then in its infancy, to be continued.

The game drew so much money in ticket admissions that Mr. Sanford bought each player and substitute of the Rice Institute and University of Colorado teams a gold Gruen watch. The Associated Press coverage of the game carried this story, including the following line in an account that went on the wires over the entire nation: "Dr. Joseph L. Cline of the local U. S. Weather Bureau played the best football of all, and was also the recipient of one of the watches."

Word of this story was the first intimation I had received of such a gift to me, and it came in the form of a clipping mailed me by a friend in the Weather Bureau office at San Francisco. The first direct information I had of it was a telephone call, shortly after arrival of the clipping, from the City Hall, where I was invited to call at the Mayor's office. A large crowd was awaiting me there, and I was duly and pleasantly presented with the watch, an event which was commemorated in a photograph taken on the spot and published in one of the Dallas papers.

Afterward, the Chief of the Weather Bureau wrote me that, under the circumstances, I might keep the timepiece, and, with considerable appreciation to Mr. Sanford, I still take great pleasure in wearing it.

Too numerous to mention them all here have been the happy incidents of my many years' service with the Weather Bureau; and there have been too many to mention who have voiced commendation of my work. Younger men whom I meet nowadays frequently tell me their fathers' views that Dallas will never again enjoy the quality of weather service that circumstances permitted me to render it. Many comment on the dropping of the "shipper's forecasts" since my retirement from active duty; these reports indicated the possible daily minimum and maximum temperatures some twenty-four to thirty-eight hours in advance of their occurrence.

Some incidents that stand out in my memory, however, I can relate. One of these had to do with my forecast, on one occasion, of the first really cold weather of the fall season, with minimum of 32 degrees. On the day following a Dallas newspaper reporter told me he had displayed his confidence in this forecast by wagering five dollars that the minimum of the morning would be the figure I prophesied. He said he had collected the bet.

The mercury stood at 80 degrees Fahrenheit on another day, when I forecasted a severe freeze which would depress the temperature to below the 18-degree mark within the following twenty-four to forty-eight hours, and telephoned the warnings to representatives of the concrete industry in Dallas. One of these, Mr. Roy Cramer, who had formerly been one of my assistants, told me about a week later that he had stopped work on a job at that time on my advice, and had encountered on his way home the foreman of another large concrete concern. The rival concern's foreman, he said, was duly warned by him, with the suggestion that the other man follow his example and leave off operations until after the prospective cold wave. The other merely retorted that "Dr. Cline doesn't know what he's talking about —a hot day like this!" and went back to his work with a snort of derision.

"Today," chuckled Mr. Cramer, "I found him digging up his frozen concrete and inquired how much money he ha l lost by not discontinuing work when he got your warnin from me. He admitted the cost of replacing the frozen m rial would be about four hundred dollars."

Mr. W. D. Garlington, a Dallas potato shipper and one of the largest dealers in carlcad lots in the country, invariably called me when he had shipments en route. If a near-zero wave was due to cross the line his shipment was to take, he unfailingly accepted my forecasts and evinced his intention of protecting his cars with extra precautions for several days of the forecast period, even though the weather, indicated by me over the telephone, was due to occur in the Northern states.

One day toward the close of winter, Mr. Garlington visited my office to thank me in person for the services I had been able to render him, remarking that his losses would have been considerable had these predictions been unavailable to him. When I commented that making accurate predictions so far in advance was a highly difficult proceeding, he said, very earnestly, "Dr. Cline, I have checked your minimum temperature forecasts, published on your shipping interests' weather card daily, for an entire winter, and, generally speaking, they were almost perfect. The average, I found, was 97 per cent of accuracy."

Indeed, many large property owners of Dallas were not backward about assuring me that, prior to establishment of the regular Weather Bureau Station, they had customarily undergone great losses resulting from hard freezes; but, they added, by following my warnings with precautionary action, these had been reduced to negligible sums. And I have reason to know that many times a single forecast of a severe freeze or warning of a forthcoming flood would insure savings in avoidance of property loss far exceeding the total of several times my annual salary.

And finally, here is how one forecast of mine played a part in the establishment of the valuable "Fruit Frost Service" for the Texas Gulf Coast:

In the month of January, 1930, an unusually cold wave, with a mass of frigid air, moved in from the North and Northwest, sliding down across Western Canada and the states south of that area. Cold wave warnings were issued south, reaching as far as Dallas and even the rarely freezing Texas Coast. Then a mass of warm air and a low barometer area formed to South-Southwest and virtually halted the mass of cold air in its southward march, whereat forecasters generally abandoned their cold wave warnings for the Southwest states.

On January 17, at six-thirty in the morning, the Dallas temperature stood at 23.4 degrees, and at Galveston the report showed the mercury at about 33 degrees. The District Forecaster for this area issued a prediction calling for stationary temperatures, and indicated that a warmer, or slightly warmer, reading might be expected on the East Texas Coast. When I, on the other hand, completed the charting of my daily weather map for that morning, I felt certain that the high pressure area to North-Northwest was increasing in intensity, and that the mass of cold air would, in fact, move rapidly southward, forcing out of its path the blockading mass of warm air. And that was what turned out to be the case.

Thus, I had differed from all forecasts issued throughout the West Gulf States. My forecast of January 17 had read: "Dallas and Vicinity—Colder. Hard to severe freeze; minimum temperature ten degrees or lower tonight." Also in my Shipper's Forecast covering a radius up to one hundred and fifty miles around Dallas during the subsequent one to two days, which was printed on the regular daily weather bulletin for Dallas and its vicinity, I wrote: "Protect shipments next 24 to 48 hours from temperatures as follows— Northward, 10 degrees below zero; East and West, 10 degrees or lower; hard to severe freeze South to Texas Coast."

This forecast was perfect, and was the only one fully calculated to put people of the West Gulf States on their guard against the severe freeze that actually occurred. For example, on the following morning, the temperature at Oklahoma City was ten below zero; that at Galveston was below twenty; at my own station, Dallas, the mercury reached three below zero.

At my request, the Dallas afternoon newspapers had published the prophecy that zero readings were probable south of Dallas.

There was a storm of criticism, directed at forecasts distributed in many places over the West Gulf States area, and some of these reached the Chief at Washington. He answered complaints with a letter, a copy of which he sent to me, quoting from my Shipper's Forecast and pointing out that the Weather Bureau at Dallas had correctly warned against a severe to hard freeze.

The spirit of criticism at Galveston was so intense that the Chamber of Commerce of that city called a special meeting to crystallize sentiment, and the Chamber's secretary was instructed to communicate with the Dallas Chamber and with the Dallas *News*, offering full Galveston support of a move to request that a Forecast Center be established at Dallas. The communication, a copy of which the *News* sent

me for comment, further stated that, if Galveston had received the forecast issued at Dallas, large quantities of ripe
strawberries, grapefruit, and winter vegetables could have
been saved. I returned the letter, enclosing with it a statement of my views that Texas needed a "fruit frost service"
for the coastal area of the state, of the type already in operation in Florida and California, and I forwarded a copy of
this report to the Chief of the Weather Bureau. I afterward
learned he had relayed this missive to the Galveston Congressional representative.

In a letter addressed to me, the Chief pointed out that
the Bureau lacked funds to establish the service in question,
and that he had so informed the Congressman, adding that
the cost would be some four thousand dollars.

And so it happened that a bill, submitted by the Representative not long after, was passed by Congress appropriat-
ing the sum needed for the purpose, and the Fruit Frost
Service was set up at Galveston. It was later moved to Houston, and finally to Harlingen, the latter city lying in the
heart of the winter vegetable and citrus belt.

CHAPTER VII

TEXAS CLIMATE—WHY DIFFERENT

The climate of Texas is renowned for its supposedly great difference from the climates of other states. This tradition has been mainly brought about by the public's general belief that it is unpredictable—by the layman, at least. For this reason, it may be interesting to have a look at the factors going to make up that much-abused element: "T e x a s Weather."

The climate of the state is affected and largely controlled by the Rocky Mountains, conditions in Plains States, valleys, and major bodies of water—among the last mentioned particularly the Gulf of Mexico, to the south. These are to a great degree the same factors that are applicable to the climate of the entire globe, which is principally governed by heat received from the sun and from the earth's interior; by the rotation of the earth on its axis; and by the mountains, hills, valleys, rivers, lakes, and seas or oceans, all of which have their elements of cause and effect upon the general movement of the encircling atmosphere.

I have often wondered if the world would have been habitable by its present forms of life had the mountains, hills and valleys been situated where the oceans and large bodies of water lie at present, and the latter situated where the land masses now stand—a complete interchange of positions between them. This is an amusing topic on which to speculate, but a wholly moot subject, since the differences resulting from such a distribution are beyond the powers of imagination.

Be that as it may, Texas has in its south portions a tropical climate, resulting from the influence of the Gulf of Mexico. It enjoys a temperate climate in its central areas. In the north part, it has its frigid climate, due to the masses of cold air moving from the North Pole towards the equator. These "northers," the name by which they are popularly known, often drive hard over western Canada, across the Rockies and Plains States into north Texas, often extending south to the Texas coast. They are actually high barometer areas, attended by cold air, which occasionally causes temperature drops of forty to eighty degrees within less than twenty-four-hour periods, as they swirl southward accompanied by their high northerly winds.

Everyone knows that cold air is heavier than warm air. When, therefore, a mass of cold air travels southward across the Rockies, it descends rapidly and spreads out over the Plains States east of the mountains. In addition, the descending air current at the center of the high barometer area brings its share of cold air downward from the upper atmosphere. The air mass moving from the mountains gathers acceleration on the downward slope of the terrain, on account of gravity's pull and the lack of resistance, there being no large forests or hills in the plains. Movement of the air may be compared to the movement of a log rolling down a steep hill; the farther it travels while meeting with little or no resistance, the greater the continuing increase in its speed.

Thus, by the time the "norther" reaches Texas, the cold air mass has picked up a wind velocity of forty or fifty miles an hour—and sometimes even greater.

All these conditions, combined with the sudden and violent nature of the disturbances, do indeed make for a somewhat different and characteristic climate in Texas, as compared with that of most other states, in which hills and forests check the movement of winds accompanying cold waves. This retardation, in turn, causes changes to seem less violent, because they are less sudden, and the resultant sensation of cold apparently less severe. This condition characterizes states much farther north than Texas, with lower general temperatures.

A story I heard told about Texas illustrates the widespread feeling about the severity of these "northers." It is said that a man who was compelled to haul his wood for a distance of several miles, reputedly left home on a hot day to pick up a load. On his way home, one of the horses hitched to the loaded wagon dropped dead from being overheated. Upon his return from seeking help in removing the carcass from the highway, he found the second horse frozen to death from a severe "norther" which had occurred during the interval.

The story went on to say that dark came on, and the man was in danger of freezing to death, in his turn, when he saw flames leaping from a bundle of logs some distance away in the woods. He ran toward the fire in shivering haste, but was so numb with cold by the time he reached it that he put his hands into the blaze. It had become so cold that the flames had frozen, and, at the impact of his hands, the blaze broke off and fell to the ground—"believe it or not."

The rotation of the earth upon its axis plays a big part in the weather movements, since high barometer areas and accompanying cold waves moving southward from the North Pole to the Equator in the Northern Hemisphere are also given an easterly trend in accordance with this rotation. If, therefore, the "norther" has moved sufficiently far to the south to enter west Texas from the vicinity of the Pacific Coast, the impact of the accompanying mass of air is not nearly, as a rule, so severely cold as that one which has crossed the northern Rockies and moved southward over the Plains States.

High and low barometer areas, as well as their offspring,

the destructive storms, tornadoes and the like, always move in the lanes wherein they encounter the smallest amount of resistance. The reader has probably observed for himself that tornadoes do their greatest amount of damage in valleys.

The most destructive and severe Texas "norther" of which the Weather Bureau has official record was the one which crossed Texas from Amarillo to the Gulf of Mexico in February, 1899. To dip further into statistics, the lowest temperature of record at Amarillo was sixteen degrees below zero, recorded February twelfth of that year. At Dallas, the readings of February twelfth and thirteenth dropped to ten below. Brownsville, in the semitropical Rio Grande Valley, had its record reading of twelve above zero. The record low temperature recorded at Galveston was seven and five-tenths degrees above, also on February twelfth. I myself took that particular morning observation, and telegraphed "shore ice" in my record, thus indicating that almost unknown phenomenon, natural frozen salt water skirting Galveston Bay.

This particular cold wave wrought more than a million dollars' worth of damage to livestock and to property generally, all across the state. The havoc it wrought among the fish in Gulf Coast waters is described in a previous chapter. The weather had been so warm and the "norther" had come so fast, that the fish feeding in bayous and inlets along the coast became chilled before they could reach the warmer deep water stretches of the Gulf. They lay numbed and helpless on the surface of the water, where they were dipped up by thousands in nets from rowboats.

An example of the sort of damage done to property, in that section so unaccustomed to having to protect itself from temperatures much below freezing, occurred in a handsome two-story residence of Galveston when a water pipe burst at its weakest point, where it ran between the ceiling of the lower story and the floor of the upper. The house was almost flooded, spreading devastation throughout. The entire ruin might have been avoided had the pipes been drained after that part lying underneath the house had frozen solidly.

In a recent conversation with a friend of mine, an attorney, on the subject of the weather, he recalled that some cattle had failed to come up from the pasture at his home near Brownwood, in West Texas, during the 1899 freeze. He related that the animals were found later, huddled together and frozen fast in an icy sheath which had formed when rain fell upon them and the nearby shrubbery, thus anchoring them to the undergrowth. The poor beasts had sought shelter in a thicket under a large tree, and the ice-covered growth was thick enough to resist their efforts to pull loose. They were chopped free from the odd trap before they were frozen to death. Had they been left there, they would have eventually been found stiff and stark, but still on their feet upheld by the growth in their icy bonds. Such sights were common in many places over North Texas during that freeze. Cattle on the open ranges drifted before the wind in search of some protecting wall until the fences finally stopped their movements. They then remained crowded together for what little warmth there might be in their own bodies, and the scant protection offered by the fences. Many newspaper reports and accounts of eyewitnesses offered proof of the fact that many cattle were found stiffly standing—although dead —against the fences of the northwest portions of Texas.

I have never been able to locate any records of a storied cold wave even more severe than the one of 1899, in the yarns spun by the oldest settlers of Galveston. Some accounts stated that a man walked across ice from one side of Galveston Bay to the other. This, as before stated, is an unsubstantiated story and its accuracy is not vouched for.

CHAPTER VIII

RECAPITULATION—REMINISCENSES OF THE PAST

And now, as I look back over the years, the parade of my life's mileposts moves past, rapidly, as it might on a short strip of motion-picture film. There were the twenty happy years spent on the farm and in the schools in Tennessee. I seem to see now as clearly as I did see them in the valleys, hills, mountains and "knobs", and woodlands I roamed in my boyhood. I taste again the Indian turnip which burned in my mouth as I ate it then. I gape once more at the captive "wild man". I am outwitting and recapturing the hogs which ran wild and had to be snared with lassoes. I am battling the mighty waves of the Gulf in the Galveston Hurricane. I am teaching again (in my thoughts), living over again my brief experience as a schoolmaster. I come to Texas—I launch upon my weather observer career—I am back in Porto Rico again—I relive my domestic happiness. Though I manage to keep active still in various types of work, I know that much of my life is over.

Summing up the impressions gained in a lifetime of experiences, I feel that today it would be well if all children living in large cities could enjoy some periods of time on farms, where almost every product of nature grows, and where they might be taught, between school semesters, the joys and mysteries of production through cultivation which does much to make rural life most worth living. That, at least, is one of the richest heritages left with me from my boyhood spent on the farm.

I have lived to see many things, some of them interesting,

some humorous and some disastrous. As related in previous chapters, some of them are burned forever into my mind, like the Galveston storm with its night of horror, but others there have been, far too numerous for publication here. A few others with the thoughts they provoked, I shall set down in this final word.

Soon after I entered Hiwassee College, a class assignment was given us, requiring that each of us write a thesis and read it before the entire student body of the school. I took for my subject a passage I had read in Sacred History which dealt with traveling in the air, and entitled my paper "Flying through the Air." In it I described how I made an imaginary set of wings, attached them to my arms and legs and, thus equipped, climbed to the top of a high bluff on the Tennessee River's bank, where there remained standing the battered stump of a tree blown down by the winds. In order to obtain a start for making a flight from this eminence, across the river and down to the opposite bank far below, I sprang into the air from this stump, which broke as my feet pushed against it, thus nullifying a good part of my initial propulsion.

Nevertheless, my glide carried me above the road at the foot of the bluff, over the bank, and out above the river, into which I subsequently splashed at a point about in the middle. The weight of my wings prevented my swimming out, and I would have drowned but for the assistance of a kind farmer who was passing on muleback along the river road. As a realistic touch, I related how my flight just over the mule caused the animal to take fright and to rear, leaving his rider in a sitting position in the dust of the road, but the latter regained his feet and came to my rescue in time to give me a hand out of the water.

Now this was in the year 1889, and flight was a power reserved, up to that time, to birds alone, so Professor Huddleston, the secretary of the faculty, asked me how such a subject had occurred to me. I told him how I derived the idea from my reading in the Bible, and from more recently reading a short news story which had appeared in a country newspaper. He was satisfied with my answer. What mankind subsequently did in giving itself "wings" through discovery and development of aviation is now history.

Now, in 1945, I have another prophecy to make. I believe that, in the not far distant future, man's inventive genius will make it possible for an individual to step out upon the roof of his home, fasten on a mechanism of some kind, and, by manipulating this device, rise into the air and glide to the roof of his office building downtown, returning home when he wills by the same mode of transportation. If my prophecy does come true, think of the relief to human traffic jams in the large cities—downward pull of gravity will be overcome.

I have had several narrow escapes. Once, while I was returning from Tennessee to Galveston after a visit home following upon my removal to Texas, I was a near-participant in a fatal train wreck near New Orleans. The train immediately ahead of us ran into an open drawbridge which was supposed to convey the traffic across Lake Pontchartrain, killing the entire train crew but sparing, without even a scratch, the lives of four hoboes who had been locked in a box car without the knowledge of the trainmen. This, I have always contended, was the one time I have known the "profession" of tramp to be bountifully paid off—and maybe it paid off "to be me", as well, in that I was riding on a passenger train, and not a certain freight train just ahead, on that day.

I was even closer to death or serious injury on another train trip, crossing northeast Texas. This wreck occurred at a track intersection of the Cotton Belt with the International

Great Northern, when a runaway freight smashed broadside into the coach wherein I was riding. I did not come out of this crash so well as did the hoboes in the previous paragraph. I was unable to walk for nearly three months, and was the recipient of nearly the most severe injuries of any of the thirty-five persons hurt.

Death was close to me more than once in Galveston. I made a narrow escape from a house which caught fire when I was sleeping, waking barely in time to flee to safety with the loss of everything except the nightwear in which I was clad. But my closest brush with the Grim Reaper resulted from the Galveston Hurricane. I hope there never will be, as history records there never was previously, such a storm and flood as was that one—yet my experience numbers several others of great severity. I was stationed at Corpus Christi when the "big flood" at Dallas took place, and the Trinity River attained a maximum stage of 52.6 feet, the highest mark of record, at six o'clock in the evening of May 25, 1908. From Corpus Christi I noted with a natural interest the various reports: water extending from Oak Cliff to the east bank of the river at a point where the Union Terminal now stands; water backed into the lowlands past the points where the protective levees now lie; water surging up to its farthest point just one block from the place where the Adolphus Hotel is situated; all traffic bridges and the railroad bridge leading into and out of Dallas washed away, leaving the only means of ingress and egress between the city and Oak Cliff that of boats. The Dallas flood second only to that one, which reached a mark of 45.8 feet at two oclock in the afternoon of April 26, 1942, fortunately did not occur until after construction of these levees, though the latter did cause maximum flood stage on that occasion to be about five to six feet higher than it would have been had the water not been contained, and prevented from flattening out over a greater area by the levees.

In Texas, where some crops are cultivated the year around, cold waves often make big news. Some of my readers may recall a severe cold wave, with temperature plummeting to a low of three degrees below zero, at Dallas on January 19, 1930, as referred to in a previous chapter. I was the first Weather Bureau official to issue and to distribute a warning that the "norther" would cross Texas, bringing zero readings to the north section of the state and subfreezing south to the coast; while at Oklahoma City, not many miles from the north border of Texas, the mercury, I said, would reach ten degrees below zero.

This warning was issued twenty-four hours ahead of the cold wave's coming. Yet some sources voiced criticism for the Weather Bureau, with the erroneous charge in letters direct to the Chief of the Bureau that the "norther" had not been forecast, and inquiring as to why it had not. Apparently these critics had not read my warning, and the forecast of the District Forecaster had not predicted such cold. Dr. Charles F. Marvin, the Chief, answered these criticisms by sending to them copies of my official forecast in proof that the blast had been accurately catalogued and foretold by me. Mine was the sole warning given in time to save or protect matured and growing crops, which made me something of the hero of the day with the farm folk.

Pronounced weather changes for the worse almost invariably brought forth a flood of telephone calls made to me personally, day or night, seeking information as to what Jack Frost or Jupiter Pluvius was likely to do next. Even today, though I have been retired and out of active Bureau work for several years, people who encounter me on the streets often tell me their parents had held me and my forecast work in high esteem. A very prominent attorney, whom I chanced to meet recently, told me that his father had fires going for a hog-killing on one occasion when I telephoned him to advise him not to kill his animals at that time. The attorney said his father promptly put out the fires, explaining that "we'll wait until Cline says it is going to be hog-killing weather."

Farmers and others to whom I had given this type of weather assistance time after time attempted to force gifts of meat, eggs, butter, fruit and vegetables upon me by way of thanks for the warnings. I attempted to prevent gifts of any kind being brought to my office or my home, and gave away to the boys who worked with me many of such proffered edibles. In declining others, I made it a point to explain to the would-be donors that we represented the Government and therefore the public, so that it was our duty to render service without remuneration other than that of our stipulated salaries.

Despite this explanation, which was, indeed, the true one, I confess to receiving a bit of thrill when well-wishers I meet at various times compliment me with such words as: "Dr. Cline, we don't get the weather service you gave us when you were in charge." I feel that these people are—perhaps in many cases for the first time, since they are no longer receiving them—genuinely able to appreciate the accurate and careful weather analyses which I furnished them.

There are many other things I should have liked to set down in this volume, including much that I have learned in my long years of studying that always fascinating subject, the weather, as well as other facts about my life and that of my family. Briefly I will say of the latter: My good wife and I reared one son, Durward Jackson Cline, Senior, who married Miss Katherine Gray. They in turn have two fine boys, Durward Jackson, Junior, and Gerald Joseph, the latter a namesake of the Biblical Joseph and of myself. I will sum up our family life in the single statement that we lived a happy and contented life, with all our essential needs provided for.

There are still a few question marks that remain as I view my life's philosophy, the result of a great many observations and experiences. One is, why does capital fight labor, and why does labor fight capital? These are seemingly two separate questions. The two, however, are really one, since each of these elements is interdependent with the other for its existence. To carry this line of thought further, it can truthfully be said that the entire human race—and, indeed, all of nature—is commonly dependent upon God and upon each other; and, when once we realize this fact, our world will become a far better place in which to live. Take the trees of the forests and the soil in which they stand as an example. The trees derive their nutrition from the earth, grow and put forth abundant leaves; those leaves fall and in their turn enrich the ground upon which the trees grow, forming a humus under their boughs throughout the forest. Such forest soil, or humus, remains moist for a longer period than does the soil of open land, retaining water better when saturated by rains.

The final result of this interchange of benefits is that forests tend to diminish the effects of floods by withholding water from the streams and thus reducing the speed of their flow, making for profit to growing plants and human life alike.

More than fifty years of my life have been spent—most of it in government service—roaming over Texas and the Gulf area, and I feel that I have achieved, or assisted in achieving, many things which have gone far toward making Texas a better place in which to live.

A man, a stranger to me, stopped me as I was walking along the street recently to ask if I were not Dr. Cline, "the weather man." I said that I was. He went on, then, to say, "I had the pleasure of meeting you on one occasion in your office, although I am sure you do not recall the incident. I travel over the Southwest and have business contacts with many business men. Let me say that I hear mention of your name more often than that of any other man in this area. You have more friends in Texas than any man I know."

This unsolicited and totally unexpected tribute from a man virtually unknown to me gratified and touched me more than words can express.

A writer once said something like this: "Human life on this gravelly ball, mystify it as you may, is a real thing. Death is the end of it, no matter if that end be marked by a humble mound or by a gorgeous mausoleum. It is the one common birthright of all." And another writer: "The boast of heraldry, the pomp of power, all that beauty, all that wealth e'er gave, await, alike, the inevitable hour. The paths of glory lead but to the grave."

And I remember, too, when I was a boy, reading some words like these: "Saturday again, another seven days gone forever; another week spent for eternal good or eternal sorrow. Have you spoken a kind word to the fallen? Have you returned thanks for blessings received, or comforted any widow's mourning spirit, or dried an orphan's tear? This is life, like some great river flowing incessantly into the sea, as does the River of Time waft the events of Today into the Oceans of the Past."

Mrs. Ula J. Cline, wife of the author, as she appeared
shortly before her death.

CHAPTER IX

LAST CHRISTMAS CARD

I copy and publish herewith the first and last Christmas card I ever wrote, with the hope that the reader will remember me when I, too, have passed away.

A CHRISTMAS REMEMBRANCE

I WISH you a Merry Christmas and
a Happy and Prosperous New Year.
May you live to see many New Years,
more prosperous than this one.

Last Christmas was a lonely and sorrowful one for me. On September 24,
1938, as the sun went down, my beloved wife, Ula Jackson Cline, the one
person who shared my life, and the
one I loved most of all, joined the
Beyond, and my heart went with her.
She was the sunshine of our home, and
an "Angel-Diamond-Pearl" on earth.
Only those who have experienced such
a loss can know what I have passed
through since that sad day.
All that is left to me now is her lovely
portrait which hangs opposite to mine
in our room—and memories. Beneath
my picture, she had framed and hung
the following beautiful and artistically
colored poem:

A FRIEND LIKE YOU
By Edgar A. Guest

A poet once this sentence penned:
"The man is rich who has a friend",
I read it and thought, "How true!
He must have had a friend like you."

To you who have thought of me in
my loneliness, I repeat the words this
Christmas: "I am your friend." Each
future Christmas Day, I would ask that
you read the poem above, and remember that I look upon you as such a friend.
Even though we should become separated by Life's uncertain ways, remember: "I am your friend."

Joseph L. Cline.

Since my sweet wife left me and passed BEYOND, I
have wished I could have gone on with her. I still hope I
may meet and be with her at the END. If I was left alone
to do something still undone, I trust my friends will help
me accomplish all things for me to do, before I pass away,
and cross the "END OF TIME."

Joseph L. Cline in later years (1943)

CHAPTER X

THE NEW WORLD

The historic line, "We are standing on the threshold of Eternity at last, as reckless of the future as we have been of the past," has been my favorite way of expressing my own ideas of existence.

I look back with pleasant memories to the "horse-and-buggy" days, when people were happy and contented and were going about their business helping others, each, in every way he could, and wearing smiles and happy-looking faces: sights we rarely see today (1944). People were honest and trusted one another in those days. There was work for everyone. The pledged word was as true as the Bible, and when a promise was given, that promise was fulfilled to the letter. There was little or no stealing where I was reared. You could once have left a new overcoat, a suit of clothes, or any piece of property in an open wagon or buggy parked on an unguarded lot in the center of Madisonville, county seat of Monroe County, or in the city of Sweetwater, Tennessee, at an early hour of the day; then have returned to that vehicle in the afternoon when you had completed the day's shopping and were ready to go home, and found everything there just as you had left it. That was the "Old World," and it was a happy one in which to live. We knew nothing about Nazism, Fascism, Newdealism, Beaurocratism, or the "New World," as it is called by some people today. But, thank God, we had justice, liberty and democracy —the Thomas Jefferson kind. The question often asked is: Will the world ever return to normal conditions? I fear that we and probably our children's children may never live to see again conditions we would call normal.

I, for one, like the horse-and-buggy days; I for one, believe we would all be much happier and more contented if we could only regain our so-called and beloved "normal" conditions—conditions similar to those of the horse-and-buggy days. Thank God I had the pleasure of living the first and happy part of my life when we had a real "democratic form of government." And as for the horse and buggy —sometimes I think automobiles and airplanes have done much toward bringing on the present World War, although changes in the form of government must have played the major part. And it is believed that we shall never have permanent peace until we have justice and fair dealings throughout the world—something we do not now have.

There have been, in this country, some erroneous beliefs about the origin of social security. Social security must have originated in Europe. I remember well upholding and praising the first social security law, which was passed by an act of Congress in 1921 under President Woodrow Wilson's administration, and which was the real beginning of social security in the United States.

At that time I told my associates in the Government service that the act was a good one and should have included all our citizens rather than merely Government Civil Service employees and workers of other specified organizations. Had all our working citizens been included in the program, we might today be in a condition approximating a heaven on earth instead of that in which we currently find ourselves. I shall always accord to the Honorable William Jennings Bryan, Secretary of State under President Wilson and a man whom I knew personally, credit for initiating social security in this country. (Incidentally, I was also acquainted with Mrs. Bryan, wife of the Great Commoner.)

The Democratic party, through an act of Congress under President Roosevelt's regime, extended "social security" so as to enable nearly all citizens to be covered by its provisions. But the original act under President Wilson's auspices is much more beneficial to those affected than the later act which extends to all.

When I came to Texas in the early Nineties I was a Democrat, but today I hardly know to what party I belong, as I am unable to discern a real Democratic Party. I hope, whatever party may be in office when the "New World" comes into existence, that this world will not be controlled by the rule of one man—a dictator. Let us all trust and pray that our beloved country, America, will some day return to "normal" conditions.

We have apparently been asleep at the wheel of the good ship, Justice. Many people believe that we have sat idly by and let most of the good things for which our forefathers fought, bled, and died pass away with the wind—never to return unless it should be after the end of time.

Perhaps this is why Joshua and some of our Presidents tried to change time. But time goes on just as God made it to go, and will so go on until time's end. It has been said, "We rise in the morning like a flower, wither with the noon-day sun—and life is done."

SUPPLEMENT

CHAPTER XI

LETTERS, ARTICLES AND LECTURES

LETTERS

Most important letters received from Chief U. S. Weather Bureau were lost in the Galveston hurricane, and I have been unable to obtain copies. I print herewith a few which show the nature of letters received from my superior officers.

Space permits the publication of only a few articles, and the most important and scientific educational lectures, which it is believed will be of interest and value to the public as well as to students and persons seeking knowledge of the subjects outlined in this book.

Government Weather Bureau Inspectors regularly inspected all field stations of the Bureau. Their duty was to visit and to examine records and make a special report on conditions of the station to Chief of Weather Bureau at Washington. Then the Chief would inform officials in charge of stations whether the inspectors' reports were complimentary or otherwise. Every letter I received from the Chief referring to inspections of my station closed with the statement, "Your station was found to be in excellent condition."

                    U. S. Department of Agriculture,
                           Weather Bureau
                         Washington, D. C.

Office of Chief Clerk.   July 20, 1899

Mr. Joseph L. Cline,
Observer, Weather Bureau,
Galveston, Texas.
(Through Official in Charge.)

Sir:
Referring to your letter of the 11th instant inclosing a paper by you on "The Use of Frost and Temperature Warnings in Protecting Fruits and Truck-gardens", and requesting authority to read the same at the annual meeting of the Texas State Horticultural Society to be held at College Station, Texas, July

25 to 29, inclusive, the Chief of Bureau directs me to inform you that you are at liberty to read this paper at the place mentioned, and to publish it if desired, but without additional expense to the United States. If published by the Texas State Horticultural Society some extra copies should be sent to the Central Office to be placed in the Library. It is possible this article would be acceptable for publication by the Department of Agriculture as a "Farmer Bulletin".

Very respectfully,

D. J. Carroll,
Acting Chief Clerk

U. S. Department of Agriculture,
Weather Bureau
Washington, D. C.

Office of Chief Clerk   August 15, 1899

Mr. Joseph L. Cline,
Observer, Weather Bureau,
Galveston, Tex.   (Through Official in Charge.)

Sir:

The Chief of Bureau directs me to return herewith the manuscript of your article on "The Use of Frost and Temperature Warnings in Protecting Fruits and Truck-Gardens", and inform you that extracts from this paper will be published in Farmer's Bulletin No. 104, which will soon be issued. Copies of this bulletin will be furnished the Galveston office for distribution, and after its publication the entire paper may be published in the newspapers of your state and vicinity, if you so desire.

Very respectfully,

H. E. Williams,
Chief Clerk.

U. S. Department of Agriculture,
Weather Bureau
Office of the Chief
Washington, D. C.

December 30, 1904

Mr. Joseph L. Cline,
Observer, Weather Bureau,
Corpus Christi, Texas.

Sir:

In answer to your letter of the 24th instant, I have to say that I am pleased to note the success that has attended your lectures in the Corpus Christi High School.

Very respectfully,

Willis L. Moore,
Chief U. S. Weather Bureau.

U. S. Department of Agriculture,
Weather Bureau
Office of the Chief
Washington, D. C.

September 27, 1905

Mr. Joseph L. Cline,
Observer, Weather Bureau,
Corpus Christi, Texas.

Sir:

I am pleased to note from your letter of the 22nd instant that you have been requested to lecture on meteorology and kindred subjects to the seniors and sub-seniors of the Corpus Christi High School. I am of the opinion that this additional work need not interfere with your official duties, and that your lectures will be appreciated and will aid in bringing about a better understanding of the meteorological work of the Government.

Very respectfully,

Willis L. Moore,
Chief U. S. Weather Bureau.

U. S. Department of Agriculture,
Weather Bureau
Washington, D. C.

November 21, 1905

Mr. J. L. Cline,
U. S. Weather Bureau Office,
Corpus Christi, Texas.

Sir:

I take pleasure in informing you that for the nine months ended September 30, 1905, you made an excellent average in both your home and outer forecasts, considerably exceeding the state forecasts in both cases.

Very respectfully,

Willis L. Moore,
Chief U. S. Weather Bureau.

QUESTIONS AND ANSWERS IN METEOROLOGY

I delivered several lectures for the U. S. Army at the Love Field and Hensley Airports on meteorological and kindred subjects, and also for the Airway Lines covering, or crossing, North Texas. In addition to other work, the Chief U. S. Weather Bureau, in telegram dated March 11, 1918, assigned me to the position of Class Instructor at Aviation School, Signal Corps, U. S. Army, Camp Dick, Dallas, Texas. Students in the Army took great interest in the work, which was very successful, many coming to the Weather Bureau Office for further information on meteorological subjects. This work was such a success that the Commanding Officer requested me to prepare a special list of meteorological questions and answers, and hold an examination for the benefit of the students. A list of questions and answers was prepared, and many copies had to be printed. After the War I met the Camp Dick stenographer, who told me I made too much work for him, as some of the men in the Army, after reaching Europe, wrote back for copies of these questions and answers, as they were considered of great value by aviation men after reaching the battle front. He said he used up several carloads of duplicating paper in furnishing copies of the questions and answers. All men in the Army at Camp Dick were picked from college and university students, which made it a high-class camp in the Army. Since that time the Weather Bureau has adopted the metric system and is trying to figure the movements of masses of hot and cold air across the country mathematically, which somewhat accounts for the weather forecasts not being as accurate as they used to be under the old system. The forecasts should improve as the weather forecasters become more familiar with weather conditions, but forecasts made mathematically will never be perfect.

The questions and answers were considered to be so valuable that they are reprinted for use of students in the public schools of today, so that they can compare Meteorology as it used to be taught with present-day teachings in the metric system.

QUESTIONS AND ANSWERS IN METEOROLOGY

Prepared by Joseph L. Cline, B.Sc., A.M., Ph.D.
Meteorologist, U. S. Weather Bureau. March 22, 1918

Q.(1): Define the science of Meteorology.
(A): Meteorology is the science which treats of the conditions of the atmosphere, its changes in condition, and the cause of conditions and changes.

Q.(2): What is the atmosphere?
(A): An envelope of gases that surrounds the earth, generally called air.

Q.(3): What properties are found in dry air at the earth's surface and what are the percentages of each?
(A): Dry air: oxygen about 21%; nitrogen about 78%; argon about 1%; and carbon dioxide about 0.03% by volume. There are traces of various other chemical substances, and air always contains some vapor of water, varying from a small amount to as much as 5% of dry air.

Q.(4): The gases in the atmosphere are a mechanical mixture; each gas has a different degree of elasticity, and the same quantity of each occupies different volumes under similar outside pressure; but each gas has the same distribution and arrangement in the air as though it alone composed the atmosphere; hence the density of the gases limits the altitude. Give the altitude of each according to known knowledge of the density of the various gases at sea level.
(A): Carbon dioxide, the heaviest, would disappear at an altitude of about 10 miles above sea level; water vapor at an altitude of about 12 miles; oxygen at a height of 30 miles; and nitrogen, of less density than others, at a height of about 35 miles. Theoretically, there should be no air at an elevation of 40 miles, but meteors, supposed to be rendered luminous by the friction of their passage through air, have been observed at a height of 100 miles or more.

Q.(5): Give three methods of reaching conclusions and deriving general laws.
(A): Inductive, deductive and experimental. The study of meteorology, to be perfect, requires the knowledge of descriptive, mathematical, and laboratory meteorology.

Q.(6): What would be the result if the atmosphere had the same temperature throughout its length, its thickness, and its breadth?

(A): It would be calm, or, in other words, there would be no wind movement.

Q.(7): From what source, or sources, does the atmosphere receive its heat that causes its movement?

(A): From the sun, and from the interior of the earth.

Q.(8): Explain how this heat affects the atmosphere.

(A): The air is composed of gases, and when gases become heated they expand. As a result, the atmosphere expands upward and outward when heated, which starts up a motion. Heavier and cooler air moves in, and the same conditions that caused the original heating and motion, if continuous, cause the cool air that moves in to be heated, and, as the air has weight, it naturally tries to seek its equilibrium; but, owing to the unequal distribution of the heat over the earth's surface, a continuous motion is caused, resulting in a movement of the atmosphere, except for short periods, over small areas where the temperature is the same.

Q.(9): Name six meteorological or weather elements.

(A): They are temperature, pressure, wind, humidity, clouds, and precipitation.

Q.(10): How do we know these elements exist in the atmosphere?

(A): We know temperature exists because thermal status of the atmosphere changes from hot or cold and vice versa as experienced by the human body, or when measured by an instrument for recording amount of heat present at time of an observation.

Pressure of the atmosphere is different at different elevations, as shown by the barometer, an instrument for measuring pressure or weight of the air; and, when a person is moving, pressure of the air against the body is noted. We know there is wind by pressure exerted. We can also see visible objects when carried by the wind, which show motion of the atmosphere. Humidity of the atmosphere is noted by the air's being more moist at times and also by the deposit of moisture when hot air comes into contact with a vessel filled with cold water; the deposit of water on the outside of a vessel filled with ice water is a deposit of moisture from the air; and deposit of moisture on window panes of a building on a cold morning when houses are heated on the inside shows the atmosphere to contain humidity. We see the clouds when vapor in the atmosphere condenses and forms water particles suspended in the air, called clouds. We know precipitation by the occurrence of rain, sleet or snow when the vapor condenses in the upper atmosphere and falls to earth; it falls as rain when condensation takes place where the temperature is above freezing, or when it falls as a water drop; when condensation of moisture in the air takes place where temperature is below freezing, we have the snowflake, if not melted in falling. Sleet and hail are frozen raindrops. (Hailstones show transition from temperature above freezing to temperature below freezing and vice versa by number of layers present in each hailstone. And the size of the hailstone depends upon the uplift of the air where the hailstones are forming.)

Q. (11): How would you prove that the atmosphere exerts 14.718 lb. per square inch at sea level under normal conditions?

(A): One cubic inch of mercury weighs 0.4906 pounds. Take a glass tube about 3 feet long, open at one end, with an area of one square inch inside. Make the bore of the tube a vacuum; then, at sea level, under normal conditions, when you insert open end of the tube in a basin filled with mercury, the column will rise 30 inches in the tube. Then the mercury in the tube is equal to 30 cubic inches and 30 x 0.4906 equals 14.718, which is the weight of the atmosphere per square inch at sea level, called "one atmosphere"; 15 lb. per square inch at sea level.

Q. (12): To what height will one atmosphere support a column of water in same tube?

(A): 33.57 feet; at sea level, water weighs about 840 times as much as the same bulk of air, and a cubic foot of air weighs about 1 1/4 ounces.

Q. (13): Does the weight of the atmosphere decrease or increase with altitude?

(A): It decreases with altitude.

Q. (14): Give approximate changes of pressure with altitude, so as to show elevation in feet and pressure in inches.

(A): The pressure decreases with altitude at the approximate rate of two inches to 1800 feet.

Q. (15): How are separate scales arranged on aneroid barometers to show changes in altitude or elevation?

(A): Separate scales on aneroid barometers are divided so that a tenth of an inch of pressure corresponds to a change of 90 feet in altitude.

Q. (16): What altitude would a person have to reach to pass approximately half the weight of the atmosphere?
(A): About 3.6 miles.

Q. (17): Would all human beings live if suddenly transferred to an altitude of 4 to 6 miles?
(A): Not all, but some might.

Q. (18): Why would they not all live?
(A): Not all can obtain sufficient oxygen through the process of breathing the rarefied air at that altitude. Persons are also affected by decreased pressure at high altitudes.

Q. (19): Give an important factor in the human organism favorable to those who can stand higher altitudes than others, and explain why.
(A): Those who have a large per cent of red blood corpuscles can ascend higher as they can obtain a larger quantity of oxygen from the rarefied air through the process of breathing.

Q. (20): If a person should descend too quickly from a very high to a low altitude what might be the possible injurious effects?
(A): It might injure or affect the ear drums, impairing hearing on account of rapidly increased pressure on outside or exposed portion of the ear drums.

Q. (21): How might injury caused by increased pressure from quick change from high to low altitude be avoided or possibility of injury to ear drums and hearing be minimized?
(A): By opening the mouth and inhaling more of the heavier air encountered while descending, so as to more nearly equalize the outward and inward pressure on the ear drums.

Q. (22): Give nomenclature of clouds and approximate altitude; also show how clouds are grouped by the International Committee.
(A): Cirrus, average altitude 5 to 8 miles.
Cirro-stratus, altitude about 5 1-2 miles.
Alto-stratus, about 3 miles. Cirro-cumulus, 3 3-4 to 4 1-2 miles.
Alto-cumulus, about 2 1-2 miles. Cumulus clouds due to ascending air currents within, top much higher than base though they are classed as lower clouds. Cumulo-nimbus clouds are the thunder and shower clouds, also classed as lower clouds. Nimbus clouds are the lower clouds from

which rain is falling. Stratus clouds are the lower clouds, like a lifted fog, just above the earth's surface.

The International Committee grouped clouds as follows:
Upper clouds: Cirrus and cirro-stratus.
Intermediate clouds: Cirro-cumulus, alto-stratus, alto-cumulus.
Lower clouds: Strato-cumulus, nimbus, fracto-nimbus.
Clouds formed by diurnal ascending air currens: Cumulus, fracto-cumulus, and cumulo-nimbus.
High fogs: Stratus and fracto-stratus.

Q. (23): Give nomenclature and position of clouds recorded by the U. S. Weather Bureau, in order of altitude.

(A): Upper clouds: Cirrus, cirro-stratus, cirro-cumulus, alto-stratus and alto-cumulus.

Lower clouds: Cumulus, strato-cumulus, cumulo-nimbus, nimbus and stratus.

Q. (24): Does the movement of clouds show the movement of the surrounding air?

(A): Generally, but not always. Often the smoke from a moving train will form one side of a triangle with the train and wind making the other two sides. Similar conditions may result in some processes of cloud formation.

Q. (25): Name two conditions that are favorable for a clear sky.

(A): There are two processes that favor a clear sky: cold winds blowing over a warm surface, and forced descending air currents. Clear skies are prevalent in North America with north or northwest winds over places covered by areas of high pressure, causing descending and outflowing air currents.

Q. (26): Give changes that generally take place in passing from a clear sky to a cloudy one.

(A): In passing from a clear sky to a cloudy one, the following changes are generally noted: first cirrus clouds thickening to cirro-stratus or cirro-cumulus and then becoming alto-stratus or alto-cumulus and then nimbus or often fracto-nimbus clouds.

Q. (27): Give changes that generally take place in passing from a cloudy to a clear sky.

(A): In clearing, nimbus clouds often break up into fracto-nimbus, through which we often see upper clouds—cirrus or cirro-cumulus. Then the upper cloud layer often disappears or changes so as to leave only fracto-nimbus, which becomes strato-cumulus, finally leaving cumulus, after which, with favorable conditions, the sky will clear.

Q. (28) : How many processes are found in the atmosphere that may lead to cloud formation?

(A) : There are nine processes that may lead to cloud formation found to exist in the atmosphere.

Q. (29) : What are the processes and recognized causes of cloud formation?

(A) : Eight of the processes that may lead to cloud formation produce condensation of the aqueous vapor in the atmosphere by cooling, and one by water vapor, as follows:

Condensation in Warm Winds blowing over cold surfaces, the temperature being reduced until condensation takes place.

Condensation in Ascending Air Currents due to convection. Rising air is cooled about 1.6 degrees F. in ascending 300 feet, and in ascending air currents the temperature is thus lowered and the capacity of the air for holding moisture is reduced until condensation takes place.

Condensation in Forced Ascending Currents—Air forced to rise will expand and become cooler until condensation may take place.

Condensation caused by Diminishing Barometric Pressure— When the pressure is reduced, air will expand and, as a result, become cooler; and in this way condensation of aqueous vapor in the atmosphere takes place.

Condensation in Atmospheric Waves—When air rises on account of the passage of waves, it expands, becomes cooler, and may go below the dewpoint and cause clouds.

Condensation Caused by Radiation—Air may radiate its heat into space or to the cold ground, and go below the dewpoint, causing clouds.

Condensation by Mixing Air—Two quantities of saturated air of different temperature mixed will result in condensation of vapor and cause clouds.

Condensation Due to Conduction—Air layers may lose sufficient heat by conduction to adjoining layers to go below the dewpoint and cause clouds; clouds thus formed are more likely to be cirrus or cirro-stratus forms.

Condensation by Diffusion of Water Vapor—A quantity of saturated air between two layers of air containing a large amount of moisture and some of the air passing to it by diffusion, thus supersaturating it, would probably cause cirrus or stratus clouds.

Q. (30) : Explain fully and tell why precipitation does not fall to earth from all clouds.

(A) : Precipitation, or water particles, when clouds form are very small water particles, and evaporation takes place when the small water drops fall into drier air below or are carried into drier air by winds. The distance the precipitation falls as a result of gravitation depends on the size of the water particles and the dryness of the air beneath. The denser the clouds, the larger the raindrops and the faster they fall, thereby reaching a lower altitude when large than when small.

Q. (31) : What difference is there in water particles in upper and lower clouds?

(A) : The lower clouds consist of rain drops or small water particles, and the upper clouds consist of snowflakes and ice needles, as proved by observations made on mountains and in balloons.

Q. (32) : Name some of the clouds known to consist of ice crystals or ice needles.

(A) : Cirrus and cirro-stratus and often cirro-cumulus.

Q. (33) : Does the wind velocity increase or decrease with elevation?

(A) : It increases.

Q. (34: Explain approximate increase of wind velocity with altitude.

(A) : Increase of wind velocity with altitude is very rapid for the first 100 to 200 feet, as the lower surface winds are retarded by friction with the earth; but, above 200 feet, the increase is slow. It is quite probable that up to some unknown altitude the wind velocity increases, and at higher altitudes decreases.

Q. (35) : Give the progressive movement of areas of high and low pressure in the northern and southern hemispheres.

(A) : They move eastward in the northern hemisphere, and westward in the southern hemisphere.

Q. (36) : What is their average progressive movement in miles across the country?

(A) : About 30 miles per hour.

Q. (37) : How does the wind move in low barometer areas, or in cyclonic disturbances?

(A) : The wind movement is spiral and circulates spirally inward with opposite motion to the hands of a watch with its dial facing upward at the surface of the earth in the northern hemisphere, and vice versa in the southern hemisphere.

There is an ascending air current at the center of the disturbance, and this circulation at high altitudes is vice versa to the circulation at the earth's surface.

Q. (38): How does the wind circulate in an anticyclone or high pressure area?

(A): Spirally outward, and with the motion of the hands of a watch with its dial facing upward at low elevations in the northern hemisphere, and vice versa in the southern hemisphere; and circulation at high or upper altitudes is vice versa to surface air currents.

Q. (39): What is the theory as to the cause of the wind movement in the two hemispheres?

(A): The theory is as follows: "If a free-moving particle (such as that of air) moves along near the earth's surface, there is a force arising from the diurnal rotation of the earth which deflects it to the right of its course in the northern hemisphere and to the left of its course in the southern hemisphere."

Q. (40): Show the amount of this influence of the rotation of the earth by example.

(A): "At latitude 50° a rifle ball moving 1700 feet per second, discharged at a target 3,300 feet distant, would deviate about 4 inches to the right of the target in the northern hemisphere and the same amount to the left of the target in the southern hemisphere. This effect, slight as it may appear, shows results of great importance when operating upon masses of air moving day after day over distances of thousands of miles.

Q. (41): Give approximate average decrease in temperature with altitude.

(A): The amount of cooling for air is approximately 1.6° F; for a rise of 300 feet, and in the case of descending air the reverse is true. The air is compressed in descending, and, as a result, a corresponding rise takes place.

Q. (42): Does the progressive movement of areas of high and low pressure across the country have anything to do with the velocity of the spiral winds around these areas of high and low pressure? If not, give short explanation of probable cause of wind velocities.

(A): No. The wind velocity depends upon the temperature and pressure gradients attending the low and high barometer areas.

Q. (43): When pressure distribution prevailing at the time,

as charted on daily weather maps, is known, give eight rules based on average conditions for predicting wind conditions likely to be encountered above the surface wind.

(A): Following are eight rules for forecasting winds aloft:

1. With a distant LOW approaching from the southwest, the surface winds are easterly and shallow, and above them is a layer about 1 kilometer in depth in which there is little or no wind; above this layer southwesterly winds prevail.

2. As a LOW passes north of the station, surface winds are successively southeast, south, and southwest, and the turning of wind with altitude is clockwise, the upper winds nearly always being southwest to west.

3. With a LOW northeast of the station and a HIGH southwest, both surface and upper winds are northwest. As this HIGH approaches and passes south of the station, the surface winds are successively west-northwest, west, and west-southwest, turning clockwise with altitude to northwest.

4. With a HIGH east of the station and a LOW approaching from the west or west-northwest, winds are southwest and strong both at the surface and aloft.

5. With a HIGH north of the station and a LOW approaching from the southwest and passing south of the station, surface winds are north-northeast to east-northeast and there is little turning up to 4,000 meters; the turning at higher levels is counter-clockwise to north-northwest and northwest.

6. With a HIGH northwest and a LOW south of the station, surface winds are north to northeast, turning clockwise with altitude to northeast, and at higher levels counter-clockwise back to north-northwest.

7. With a HIGH on the northwest and a LOW passing northward east of the station, surface winds are successively north-northwest and northwest, turning counter-clockwise with altitude to northwest and west-northwest.

8. In general, the turning of winds with altitude is usually such that they have a westerly component before the 3-km level is reached.

Q.(44): Give character of the approaching weather changes afforded by local observations of the wind and the barometer.

(A): When the wind sets in from points between south and southeast and the barometer falls steadily, a storm is approaching from the west or northwest, and its center will pass near or north of the observer within twelve to twenty-four hours, with winds shifting to northwest by way of southwest and west. When wind sets in from points between east and northeast and the barometer falls steadily, a storm is approaching from the south or southwest, and its center will pass near or south of the observer within twelve to twenty-four hours, with winds shifting to northwest by way of north. The rapidity of the storm's approach and its intensity will be indicated by the rate and amount of the fall in the barometer.

GENERAL INFORMATION

By bearing in mind the usual movements of lows and highs. and the conditions that accompany them, coming weather changes may be foretold from the weather charts. Of course, the question of topography and the location of land and water areas with regard to the place for which the prediction is made are most important factors, and a person of limited experience should not expect to make altogether satisfactory forecasts without considering these and other important influences.

Often a close student of clouds and cloud formation can get a good idea of approaching weather conditions, especially rain, by observing weather conditions in the west at sunset.

For knowledge of aeronautical terms, see copy of little pamphlet entitled "SKY WORDS," copyrighted by the Vacuum Oil Company, New York, New York.

There are three ways of natural movements which produce rain.

(1) Air rising like a bubble and producing cumulus and cumulo-nimbus clouds.

(2) Air going upwards as a current, moving up a slope over the cold air.

(3) Cold air going under warm air and pushing the warm air up.

Origin of Thermometers

We are taught the Fahrenheit thermometer originated at Danzig in 1714; mercury was used for the fluid, and the two known temperatures——the freezing and boiling points of water ——which had previously been employed by Huyghens in 1665 were utilized to give the graduation.

The Centigrade scale was introduced by Celsius and Linnaeus at the University of Upsala in Sweden, 1742.

The Reaumur thermometer scale was produced by the French physicist of that name in 1731, although the Reaumur and also the Centigrade were later somewhat modified by others.

The foregoing meteorological questions and answers were written after a close study of textbooks on Meteorology by Ferrel, Abercromby, Davis, and Waldo; these authors were among the leading meteorologists at that time.

Prior to the establishment of the U. S. Weather Bureau, people formed ideas of approaching weather by observing clouds and noting actions of birds, insects, and animals. And today, certain types of clouds at sunset, and actions of some insects, birds, and animals warn people of coming weather changes, prior to their being forcasted by Government weather forecasters.

WEATHER CONDITIONS WHICH OFTEN GIVE RAIN AND STATIONARY TEMPERATURE ON THE TEXAS COAST DURING WINTER WHEN MOST FORECASTERS EXPECT FAIR AND COLDER WITH FROST TO EXTEND SOUTH TO TEXAS COAST

By Joseph L. Cline, Observer, U. S. Weather Bureau,
Corpus Christi, Texas—1904

A daily weather map which convinces the Forecast Official that a certain forecast will be verified before said forecast is issued, does not present any interesting meteorological features for study, because no new theories, or laws, are likely to be produced by the study of such maps.

I spent more than ten years of my service in the U. S. Weather Bureau on the Texas Gulf Coast, and it has been a great pleasure to note and study weather types produced on daily weather maps that give different results from those often forecast by the best forecast officials in the Bureau.

In my article on "Weather Forecasts and How to Improve Them," written and submitted several years ago in the competitive test for a professorship in the U. S. Weather Bureau, I called attention to conditions that cause rain during certain periods of the year over the states bordering on the Gulf of Mexico, while, during other periods, the same conditions would give fair weather, i. e., a high barometer, or anti-cyclonic disturbance, over Atlantic and east Gulf states and a low barometer, or cyclonic disturbance, over the northwest portion of the country. A description of these conditions was used in said article to show that forecasts could be improved by a closer study of weather types and resulting weather phenomena, and I am more fully convinced of this fact today than I was at that time. Since then I have watched conditions closely: I have a personal file of certain weather types that cause rain and stationary temperature on the west Gulf coast during the winter season when the U. S. Weather Bureau Forecast Official generally forecast fair and colder weather with frost to coast.

The daily weather maps of January 13 and 27, 1902, and January 26 and February 19, 1904, are very good types, showing meteorological conditions that give precipitation on the Texas coast when fair weather was forecast, and they are re-

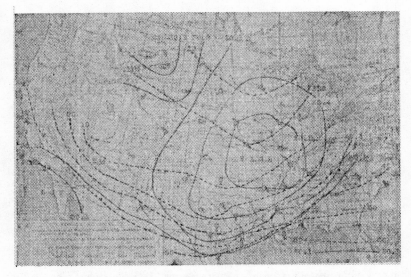

Weather chart showing average meteorological conditions over the United States that give rain and stationary temperature on the Texas coast during winter seasons, when weather forecasters forecast fair and colder with frost to Texas coast.

ferred to for the information of those who may wish to study these conditions.

The conditions shown on map of January 13, 1902, gave rain on the Texas coast the following night and all next day, and the rain area moved east with the progressive eastward movement of the area of high pressure that was central over the lower Mississippi Valley. A barometric disturbance moved in over the west Texas coast on the following day. The map of January 27, 1902, shows the area of high pressure farther north. These conditions gave rain over the greater portion of the southern states for two days, prior to the appearance of a barometric disturbance in the Gulf off the east Texas coast. Telegraph reports failed to outline the disturbance in the Gulf until it moved inland near Galveston, Texas. Temperature and weather forecasts issued on the above maps were not verified, and the daily maps of January 26 and February 19, 1904, show similar results. On the latter map a barometric disturbance was noted in the east Gulf, which increased in intensity and gave a falling barometer and general rainstorm along the Gulf coast, instead of moving eastward and being followed by a rising barometer and fair weather.

When barometric conditions like those under discussion exist, there is generally a disturbance in the Gulf of Mexico, and frequently the relative positions of the area of high and low pressure give steady northeast winds on the Texas coast. Such conditions prevail so often during winter that the inhabitants have taken note of it. When the wind shifts to the northeast, they say, "Look out for rain. The wind is from the right quarter." Once, during a severe winter drouth, the wind remained from the northeast and east for nearly two days, without even producing cloudy weather, and the farmers claimed that there was something wrong with the elements. Their winter cabbage crop was suffering from want of moisture and naturally, they were watching the conditions closely.

It is believed that forecasts for the Gulf states could be materially improved by establishing two floating meteorological stations in the central part of the Gulf of Mexico; one south-southeast of Corpus Christi, Texas, and the other south of Alabama or eastern Louisiana. These stations would show barometric disturbances in the Gulf when they existed; and, during the hurricane season, they would be of inestimable value in determining the probable course of West India hurricanes.

Weather charts that frequently give opposite results from the forecasts issued for the west Gulf coast during winter, generally outline an area of high pressure, accompanied by clearing and much colder weather, moving southeastward over the states east of the Rocky Mountains, with crest over Kansas and western Missouri; or the central Mississippi Valley, and barometer low over the Gulf of Mexico with slight barometric disturbances central over the extreme southwest and northern Rocky Mountain region. Another area of high pressure is occasionally shown to be moving in over the extreme northwest portion of the United States. Clear weather extends southward over central Texas, Arkansas, and West Tennessee, while it is cloudy with rain still falling in scattered places over the southeastern states. Reports show cloudy weather on the Texas coast; and, as it is clearing with the progressive eastward movement of the area of high pressure, which appears to predominate in the weather over the greater portion of the country, the Forecast Official believes that it will clear on the west Gulf

coast during the day. And, as rain has generally ceased falling
west of the Mississippi river, he issues a forecast for following
36 hours calling for fair and colder weather, with frost on
the Texas coast on the following morning; but about eight
times out of ten it is raining or sleeting on the Texas coast
within 24 hours, especially if conditions remain about the same.
It is common during winter for rain to fall over south Texas
when the 8:00 p. m. meteorological reports show a barometer
two- to three-tenths inch higher at Palestine, Texas, than at
Corpus Christi, Texas, with cloudy weather over the greater
portion of the state. These barometers will occur with weather
types like those under discussion. Rain can safely be forecast for
the Texas coast on all weather charts during winter season when
these conditions prevail, and the rain area frequently moves
eastward and extends northward over Texas into Arkansas,
with the progressive eastward movement of the area of high
pressure.

During the past winter I issued practice forecasts for Fort
Smith, Arkansas, and a greater number of said weather forecasts were verified than those issued on the daily weather map
for that portion of the state covering the same period. During
five months 30 differing forecasts were issued, and all but six
were verified. Amarillo, Texas, was recently assigned to me
for practice forecast work, and during April and May of this
year my practice forecast for Amarillo differed from the state
weather forecast issued for that locality 16 times, and all but
one of the differing forecasts were verified. During the first
five months of the year 1904, the weather forecast I issued for
Corpus Christi and vicinity differed from the state forecast for
the same locality 35 times, and all but three of the differing
forecasts were verified. These differing forecasts of the weather
were based on weather types, and are given to show the relative
value of such forecasting.

From a special study of the weather types that give rain and
stationary temperature on the Texas coast when fair and colder
weather with frost is often forecast, it is observed that there
is generally a barometric disturbance to the south or southwest
of Texas which is not always within range of reports received;
hence the Forecast Official cannot note such conditions, else
his forecasts might be different. Frequently areas of low pressure move in over Texas from Mexico or the west Gulf within
two days after the types under discussion appear over the United
States. Taking this into consideration, it is believed that these

rains are caused by the warm ascending air currents in the center of barometric disturbances central over Mexico or the west Gulf, which are not always shown on the daily weather charts. These high temperatures would naturally carry up a large amount of moisture. Then these air currents drift north or northeastward toward the area of high pressure, as they ascend into the upper strata of the atmosphere, and the high temperature is lowered by the adiabatic and thermodynamic changes that are necessarily taking place. This lowering of the temperature reduces the capacity of the atmosphere for retaining moisture, and as a result the moisture is condensed and falls to the earth in the form of rain, sleet or snow, the character of precipitation depending on the temperature.

CLIMATE—AGRICULTURE

Joseph L. Cline, Weather Bureau

The prosperity of a nation, or of any country, primarily depends upon its climate, soil, inhabitants, and industries.

Climate is one of the most important features of any country. It is nearly as important a part of the environment of animal life as it is of the vegetable or plant existence. Soil can be changed artificially, without much expense, so as to be made very productive, if soil is all that is desired; but an unfavorable climate may be considered unchangeable and will probably remain undesirable forever; though often some scientists assert "Weather conditions are changing." There have been changes, or fluctuations, with periods of hot and dry, and wet and cold weather during all ages, and a "perfect climate" does not exist.

But when records covering long periods of time are studied closely, we find that climate is neither stable, nor becoming progressively drier, wetter, hotter, or colder, and it appears that weather changes in historic times have been overgeneralized. Sometimes weather conditions indicate or represent cycles covering a few to several years, with number of years not well defined. Records show periods of dry and wet weather nearly everywhere, and this condition will likely prevail as long as time lasts. It is believed that the seven fat years and the seven lean years of famine in Egypt, foretold by Joseph, as proclaimed in sacred history (Genesis XLI) as the interpretation of King Pharaoh's dream, represented cycles, or periods, of seven years with abundant rain for crops, followed by seven years of dry weather and crop failures. Somewhat similar weather conditions frequently occur in localities in this age, but with improved farming implements, intensive cultivation, and conservation of subsoil moisture, as outlined by the U. S. Department of Agriculture, better crops can be produced with less rain or moisture; hence cycles, or long periods of dry weather, are not so noticeable and so disastrous as those in the days of King Pharaoh. This is why some writers erroneously declare the climate to be changing.

When the climate and soil of different localities are known, it is, to some extent, safe to assume that plants which will thrive in one place can often be successfully transplanted to another which is similar; and in studying these matters, experimenting is in a great measure done away with. Almost any character of climate and soil can be found within the boundaries of the United States, and the inhabitants and their industries, or occupations, have made this country one of the leading nations of the world. But, in order to keep pace with other nations, it is necessary to watch economic conditions closely, try to live more at home, and overcome business depressions. In this country, with all its wealth, resources, industries, and industrious inhabitants, business depressions should be a thing of the past.

Agriculture has been an important and necessary occupation through all ages, or since the creation of man. It is the leading industry, and is apparently the basis of prosperity, of the United States. It has been said that almost all the wealth of the world comes from "Mother Earth;" hence all natural and agricultural possibilities should be cherished.

The writer, reared on a farm, realizes that successful farming requires much knowledge and hard work. Farmers, to succeed, must have sufficient education to outline and plan their work so as to surmount many obstacles and be prepared to cope with the environments surrounding their plantations, which requires a better education and more knowledge of business than many other occupations.

There is do doubt that the U. S. Department of Agriculture has done more to advance scientific farming than any other agency. By request to the Honorable Secretary of Agriculture, Washington, D. C., the farmer can obtain bulletins explaining how to enrich soils, how to combat and destroy crop pests, and how to plant, protect, cultivate, and successfully raise any farm product; and also information as to saving and marketing crops after maturity. But, with all this information and all possible legislation, farming, to be successful, must be accomplished by the farmers. No agency, or nation, can successfully help the farmers unless the individual farmers help themselves. We are taught in history that "God helps those who help themselves." Such was intended when man was thrown out of the Garden of Eden, as God said, "In the sweat of thy brow shalt thou eat bread." (Genesis III:19.)

Success in farming was recently well put as the wisdom of "safe farming" by Dr. C. W. Warburton, Director of Extension Work and Secretary of the Drouth Relief Committee, in outlining progress of relief work in the South, when he said, "Seldom has it been so clearly demonstrated that ample supplies of foodstuffs for the family and feed for the farm animals must be a first consideration in planning the season's cropping program."

Farmers who produce only cotton, corn, wheat, or one crop, so to speak, may succeed in a good crop year, when the product can be sold for more than the cost of production. But those who diversify, raise a little of every farm product that can be successfully grown on their plantations, and live at home, are generally the most prosperous and best contented agriculturists.

Farmers, as a rule, are most successful when they raise their own vegetables; cultivate some corn, cotton, wheat, oats, and other adaptable staple farm products; put out a small fruit orchard; raise some chickens, turkeys, ducks, guineas, and livestock, such as hogs, cattle, sheep, and goats; and also cultivate feed for farm animals. Then, when going to the market, they should always take some surplus farm product, such as eggs, chickens, butter, etc., to sell, so as to pay for needed articles not produced on the farm. After such articles have been purchased, it is believed that by economy, systematic farming, and marketing surplus farm products each year, there would be some cash saved for a rainy day or a bad crop year.

Surplus vegetables, fruit, and other perishable farm products can be canned, preserved, pickled, or saved in some manner, so as to have something to live on throughout the year. Potatoes, onions, and apples, spread out on wooden boards or planks in a cool, dry cellar, will keep for several months, especially during the winter season. Turnips, cabbage, and potatoes can be kept fresh most of the winter, if carefully harvested and placed in a shallow hole in the ground, piled up like a mound to a cone-like top above the ground, and then covered with hay or straw, with about five or six inches of loose dirt on top of the hay or straw, and a sloping plank roof put on top of the dirt so as to keep water out. They can be taken out as needed during the winter through a temporary opening or door on one side of the mound. Cabbage can also be put up for home use by making homemade sauerkraut.

Co-operative, or community, farming can be made very convenient, in the following manner: One or more farmers buy a gristmill for grinding corn, a small canning outfit for canning fruit and vegetables, and a canemill and evaporation pans for making syrup, to be used by all farmers in a neighborhood in a manner somewhat similar to the custom of wheat threshing.

Fresh meat can be made available for home use by a number of farmers working together. One farmer may kill a beef or mutton one week and divide with his neighbors; another may kill and divide during another week; and so rotate around until each farmer has furnished all others in the company with about an equal quantity of fresh meat.

Co-operation in raising and marketing crops, so as not to flood the market after harvesting, will prove beneficial. If producers sell only a portion of each staple crop, or product, as it becomes matured and ready for market, and hold some for sale during other seasons of the year, there will likely be a more stable market and better marketing prices for most products.

Labor is an important factor in a successfully managed farm. It is necessary to have farm hands, or tenant farmers. Each tenant farmer or married employee should be furnished a comfortable home, with a place to raise chickens, etc., and be given a small tract of land on which to raise vegetables and food stuffs for his family and necessary farm animals. If employees are given Saturday afternoon of each week off to cultivate their garden truck, including a roasting-ear patch, and to look after their personal affairs, it would result in better farming and make it easier to keep good tenants and farm employees.

Some farmers solve the problem of keeping their boys interested in farming, so that they will be better contented and remain at home, by giving each son one field of wheat, corn and cotton, and letting him cultivate, harvest, and sell his individual crop, keep the money, and be permitted to buy and feed a few beef cattle for the market each year. This goes a long way toward keeping farm boys interested, and teaches them how to trade, save, and be successful.

Every plantation should have good barns and outhouses for sheltering livestock, protecting farm implements, and storing foodstuffs, especially during the winter seasons. By having farm implements stored when not in use, during periods of rainy and bad weather unfit for outdoor work, all machinery can be repaired, oiled, and put in good condition, and will last longer and be ready for use when needed. Fences can be built and repaired, and much other farm work can be done during periods of weather unfavorable for crop cultivation. Success of farming, as well as of other industries, depends largely upon ability of the manager to keep everything moving, so that no time, money, or property will be lost or wasted.

The writer was reared on a farm, with poor soil, which was operated and managed by methods similar to those outlined in this article. The owner of the farm was thrown out on the world at the age of twelve when his father died. He started barefooted without a dollar, and worked hard at first as a hireling, then as a tenant farmer; and later bought a farm. At the age of fifty-six, he was able to retire, and the income from rents of his farm comfortably kept him and his wife until they passed away.

Even after farmers have faithfully completed their task of diversification, raised bountiful crops, and lived at home, a nation can not prosper unless the Government, every citizen, and every business firm or industry lend a helping hand. There should be a surplus of marketable crops over and above products consumed on the farms, as farmers should have something to sell, so that they can obtain sufficient funds to purchase machinery to operate the farms and buy necessities of life, such as clothing, coffee, salt, pepper, sugar, etc., that cannot be produced on all farms. A surplus is also needed for other citizens, and for operating other industries in promoting prosperity. Then it is up to the bankers, wholesale, retail, and produce merchants, manufacturers, and every citizen of the nation, and the Government, to see that producers can dispose of their surplus at a living profit. The Government can have laws for the protection of its citizens, but it is necessary for every citizen to honor and stand by the Government, obey the laws, and protect and assist every other citizen. Every inhabitant must possess vision and knowledge to assist the Government, farmers, individuals, and all industries in passing through economic changes vitally necessary for the development, prosperity, and happiness of a nation. Citizens can get out of a Government, industry, occupation, or life only what they put into it; and with every citizen obeying the injunction, "Do unto others as you would have them do unto you," or "Live and let live," this world of ours will be a much better place in which to live. A successful and prosperous Government should never destroy farm or other products, but, instead, it should find a market at home, or in other countries for all the surplus commodities produced or manufactured; and then prosperity, peace, and happiness will always be with us. It should be the duty of our Government to uphold "Reciprocity": namely, to let foreign countries ship in their surplus products that we do not produce, free of traiff, provided they will let us ship to them our surplus products—a plan which will have a tendency to bring the world together as one big family.

One prominent farmer who read this lecture soon after it was written said he had cotton gins in 32 counties in Texas, and wanted to make photostatic copies and furnish one to every farmer in every county where he had gins. Also a statistician for one of the most prominent institutions in the United States read this article, and stated that it was the best article on agriculture that had ever been written.)

RAINFALL AND FORESTRY

Verbatim report of an address by Dr. Cline, which is self-explanatory, as published in the Dallas *Morning News,* November 24, 1918, follows:

DISCUSSES EFFECT OF TREES ON RAINFALL

Address of Dr. Cline Before Forestry Association Is Given

One of the most interesting addresses made at the fourth annual convention of the State Forestry Association in Dallas Thursday, in the opinion of officers of the association, was "Rainfall and Forestry," by Dr. Joseph L. Cline, B.Sc., A.M., Ph.D., local Weather Observer. It was the wish of the officials that the address be published in full, so that the general public may learn of the value of forests in regard to the supply and distribution of rainfall.

The address of Dr. Cline follows:

The question of rainfall and forestry as referred to by the honorable president of this association is one of great importance and one that requires much thought and study. Many able writers believe the two factors, rainfall and forestry, are linked or woven together and depend upon each other. It is true the forest areas, to a great extent, outline the rainfall area of a country. We find forests where there is rain, or vice versa. The largest and most perfect forests were found by the earliest settlers of all new countries to be where the rainfall was the greatest. The greatest of all forests are claimed to be in the rainy tropics, as in the Amazon region, the trees being interlaced with vines and covered with air plants. In the United States the early settlers considered the forests along the Atlantic coast as an enemy of agriculture and a detriment to the quick settlement of the country. The timber made it necessary to clear the land before settling. We might truthfully say too much timber caused a lack in appreciation of forestry by the early settlers of this country. This has resulted in a waste and wanton destruction of forests by the present generation. The forests along the Atlantic States show the increased rainfall as the annual precipitation increases from the Rocky Mountains eastward to the Atlantic coast.

The greatest annual precipitation in the United States is slightly more than 100 inches in portions of Washington and Oregon, and wood is, by far, the most important product of the coast forests of the aforesaid states. The fact that forests and rainfall areas are always found linked together has caused many writers to claim forests cause rain, but it is believed that the primeval forests were the result of rain instead of the rainfall being caused by the forests. It is true that after forests are established the humus, or forest soil, remains moist longer than open land. Snow will remain unmelted on the ground in the forests from ten to fifteen days after the snow has disappeared from open fields. This humus, or forest soil, must become water-soaked after dry weather before much water will flow off, and as a result forests naturally have a tendency to diminish floods by holding moisture and causing a slower stream flow. Where forests abound there is little washing or erosion of the soil; it is estimated that a billion tons of fertile earth have been taken to the seas every year by washing.

Forests Cause Rain

There is an apparent reason for some writers to believe that forests cause rain. The transpiration or passage of water through trees and plants to the free air is enormously great. An area covered with plants will give five times as much water vapor to the free air as the same area covered with water, and twelve times as much as that from a similar land surface area during the same time. But no matter how much moisture there is present in the air, atmospheric conditions must be favorable for the condensation of the moisture before precipitation will occur. Atmospheric air always contains more or less vapor of water, varying from a small quantity to about five per cent of the amount of dry air. If all the water vapor present in the air could be condensed at one time and fall as rain, it would not amount to much more than 2.50 inches. Half of the water vapor in the air lies below the altitude of about 6,500 feet, while half of the air lies below the altitude of about 18,000 feet. Owing to the low altitude of the greater portion of moisture in the atmosphere, mountains exert a powerful influence in the distribution of moisture over the earth's surface.

The semiarid regions of the United States are, no doubt, the result of mountainous conditions and the natural eastward movement of high and low barometer areas, with their attending weather conditions, instead of being due to the lack of forests. When an area of low pressure, with its attending warm, moist air, ascends the western slope of the Rocky Mountains, condensation of the moisture usually takes place by the cooling of the air coming into contact with the colder mountain top or by adiabatic cooling of the ascending air, or by both, often causing precipitation on the western slope of the mountains. Then the air, with its moisture thus abstracted, begins its descent east of the mountains much drier; its adiabatic increase in temperature as it moves down the mountain is more rapid than the adiabatic cooling in its ascent, and with the descent the relative humidity decreases as the temperature rises. When the air reaches the base of the mountains it is warmer and drier. As a result, the ascending air currents in areas of low pressure will not produce or cause as much rain near the mountains as similar barometric conditions will farther eastward, after the spiral winds around the low barometer areas have carried more moisture inward to the center of the "low," making conditions more favorable for rain as the low barometer areas move eastward from the Rocky Mountains toward the Atlantic coast. This accounts for the small normal amount of rainfall just east of the Rocky Mountains. To change the semiarid conditions of the West, it is believed that it would be necessary to change the topography of the country or change the movement of high and low pressure areas across the continent.

Distribution of Rain

It is a mooted question as to the effects of forests upon the distribution of rainfall over the country; however, forests do add much to the happiness and prosperity of a nation. They furnish material for building homes and wood for keeping the homes warm and comfortable. The forests also furnish cool and shady places for both man and beast. Even the aviator, when soaring, can tell whether he is passing over a forest, a water area, or an open country by the air currents encountered.

Forests play an important part in retarding the movement of the atmosphere near the earth. The yield of crops can be increased in many places by planting trees for windbreaks. Where trees are planted for this purpose, they should be set zigzag, so that the wind will pass through the rows by going around the trees, thus retarding the direct movement of the velocity of the winds. When trees are set in solid straight rows, the atmosphere will rise, pass over the trees, then descend to the earth's surface and move on with slight, if any retardation, because no counter air currents are produced or caused by such windbreaks.

The forests, mountains, and rigid land surfaces of the earth retard the movement of the atmosphere by friction and resistance much more than the mobile water surfaces; and, if it were not for these natural conditions, constructed by Providence, there would be constant higher and probably more destructive winds. The value and importance of forests to civilization has never been appreciated by the general public. It is hoped the American people, who, on account of abundance and prosperity, are prone to waste, will soon awake and realize the great necessity for the conservation of forests. When our natural forests become depleted, there will be no wild birds or game, as their homes will be destroyed and the beauty of nature will be no more.

A friend of mine who had read the above address on "Rainfall and Forestry," in speaking to me one day about it, said: "Dr. Cline, that was an able address. It contained valuable information, many instructive ideas applicable to Meteorology and Forestry; and that is why the Governor of Texas selected and appointed you as one of the fifty prominent men of Texas to meet and outline a program to submit to the Texas Legislature for the purpose of establishing a 'State Forestry Law.' You have done much good work to help make Texas a better place in which to live. We need more men like you, always doing something for the good of the country."

THE CLIMATE OF TEXAS IN ITS RELATION TO THE CULTIVATION OF THE OLIVE

By Joseph L. Cline, B.S., Observer, U. S. Weather Bureau

The following paper on "The Climate of Texas in Its Relation to the Cultivation of the Olive," by Joseph L. Cline, B.S., Galveston, Observer, United States Weather Bureau, was read at the annual meeting of the Texas State Horticultural Society at Bowie, Texas, on July 31, 1895, by permission of the Chief of the United States Weather Bureau:

Mr. President and members of the Texas State Horticultural Society: It affords me much pleasure to address you on this occasion. The subject selected for my discourse is one of great interest to the people of this state, and I hope that the reading of this paper will have a tendency to open a new field in your line of work in Texas. The olive, when it can be successfully cultivated, is one of the most remunerative products which can be grown, and during the past few years I have been studying the possibility of its cultivation in southern Texas and have also endeavored to determine by comparison of climatic conditions the varieties which might be adaptable to this climate and soil. Climate must be taken into consideration when contemplating the introduction of any plant. The soil can be changed artificially without very great expense, but an unfavorable climate will probably remain so forever; hence the horticulturist as well as the farmer, before settling in a new country, should thoroughly acquaint himself with the climate and see whether it is suitable for his occupation and health. To learn what products are best adapted for cultivation in the various portions of a country by experimenting requires an ordinary lifetime, and, as we are living in a fast age, man can not afford to lose so much valuable time. When the climates of various localities are known, it is safe to assume that plants which will thrive in one can be successfully transplanted to another which is similar, and by the study of these matters experimenting is in a great measure done away with.

In discussing the climate of Texas we have such an immense area of territory to deal with that it would require a volume to bring out all the climatic features of the state, hence I will refer briefly to those conditions which have the greatest influence on the cultivation of the subject under consideration. The state contains within its boundaries one-eleventh of the United States, Alaska excluded, and the climate varies considerably, partaking of the tropics in the south, and the temperate regions in the north. It is found from the records that January is the coldest month in the year and gives the lowest temperatures generally, although over the Panhandle the minimum is often deferred until in February. In a paper which I have just published, entitled "Normal Temperatures and Precipitation in Texas" (special bulletin No. 5 of the Texas weather service), I found that the lowest monthly mean temperature was 31.6 degrees at Fort Elliott, Wheeler County, in January, and the next lowest was 33 degrees in Hartley, Hartley County, in February. These stations are located in the Panhandle, and as we proceed southward the temperature rises rapidly until the coast is reached, where the average temperature in winter ranges from 52 to 57 degrees. The temperature generally ranged from 15 to 30 degrees lower over the northern portion of the state in the winter than over the southern portion, while in summer the difference is comparatively small. The extreme range in the normal temperature during the summer months does not exceed 10 degrees.

Temperatures above 100 degrees have never been experienced along the immediate coast, while generally over the northern and central portions of the state such temperatures are experienced during the summer, especially in June, July and August; but such temperatures have been experienced in other states much farther north than northern Texas. The highest temperature in the 'state of which there is any record is 115 degrees, which occurred at Panter (Granbury P. O.), Texas, Hood County, on July 3, 1894, during the prevalence of "summer hot winds." Temperatures of this character are rarely observed, as hot winds seldom occur in the state, especially over the southern portion.

Temperatures below freezing are rare and of short duration along the immediate coast, and during the past twenty-three years there have been five in which the temperature did not fall to freezing and one in which the mercury just reached the freezing point. The lowest temperature which has occurred since the records have been kept at Galveston was 11 degrees on January 8, 1886. It was reported on this occasion that the Galveston bay froze over, and this was probably the severest norther ever experienced along the immediate coast. The temperature falls much lower with a norther over the northern portion of the state, but there the mercury rarely ever falls be-

low zero; and, when temperatures near zero do occur, they are
of short duration, lasting from one to three days only.

Frosts play an important part in the cultivation of fruits and
vegetables, and I hope that in the near future the horticulturists
will be able to utilize the frost warnings which are issued by
the United States Department of Agriculture, Weather Bureau,
in protecting their fruits. I understand that the chief of the
Weather Bureau has the mechanism of a frost annunciator of
some kind under contemplation, which, when put into operation, will be of great benefit to the horticulturists.

In special bulletin No. 5 of the Texas weather service, with
reference to frosts, it is stated that the average date of the first
killing frost in autumn ranges from October 15 over the extreme northern portion of the state to December 25 along the
immediate coast, and the last killing frost in spring ranges from
February 5 over the southern portion of the state to April 1
over the northwestern portion. From these data it is observed
that there is only about one month during the winter in which
killing frosts occur over the coast district, a condition which
proves very favorable for the cultivation of many semitropical
plants and makes a very favorable climate for a winter health
resort. Winters over the coast district are rare in which more
than three or four frosts occur, and frequently but one severe
frost is experienced, or none at all. During the past twenty-
four years there have been five winters without frost and six
with only a single frost along the immediate coast.

The character of the winds, especially the prevailing direction, will play an important part in connection with the cultivation of the olive in Texas, as will be observed later on in this
discussion. Southerly winds prevail over the southern portion
of the state, except in December and January, when the northerly winds predominate to some extent. Northerly winds prevail over the northern portions of the state during the months
of December, January and February, but there are occasional
interruptions with southerly winds in these months, and southerly winds prevail during the other months of the year. The
winds of Texas have been thoroughly studied by Prof. Mark
W. Harrington and treated in an interesting paper entitled
"Texas Monsoon," read before the Philosophical Society of
Washington, and published by that society in Bulletin, Vol.
12, pp. 293-308. In speaking of southerly winds or summer
monsoons, Prof. Harrington says: "These first appear distinctly
in March, when they occupy the territory south of a line drawn

from Texarkana to the mouth of the Pecos river. Their eastern limit is not well defined, either in this or succeeding months. In April the territory occupied by them is somewhat larger. It now lies to the southeast of a line drawn from Fort Sill, in the southwestern part of the Indian territory, to the mouth of the Pecos. In May it extends to a meridian perhaps fifty miles westward and swells northward until it reaches the Dakotas, Minnesota and Wisconsin; in June it extends fairly to the dominion boundary. From June to September it remains about the same. In October it is as in May, and in November it disappears. It is most extensive from May to October, when it occupies a territory of 10 degrees of longitude (about 500 miles) wide and 15 degrees of latitude (about 1000 miles) long."

In summarizing his paper Prof. Harrington says:

"The air flows northward from the western part of the Gulf of Mexico from March to October, and in summer reaches our northern boundary (United States) along a strip about 10 degrees wide. It flows south during the winter in Texas, but is subject to sudden accessions called 'northers,' due to cyclonic or anti-cyclonic action. This action also frequently disturbs the summer south winds, and the latter are reinforced by winds prevailing during their season in the gulf. These winds play a very important part in the climate of all Texas except the extreme west. The southerly winds (or southeasterly toward the central or western part of the state) bring coolness and comfort with them in the very season coolness is most needed.

"The north winds or winter monsoons are not so favorable for Texas, but at the same time are not less favorable than are the prevailing westerly winds over the states far to the north of it. The norther is an occasional phenomenon, not more common than the 'cold wave' of the upper Mississippi valley. Severe and destructive northers are quite exceptional."

The precipitation in the state is generally well distributed throughout the various months of the year, and it is found that the isohyetals, or lines of equal annual rainfall, traverse the state in a northerly and southerly direction. The annual rainfall is about fifty inches over the extreme eastern portion of the state, and decreases at the rate of about one inch in fifteen to twenty miles until the western portion of the state is reached, where the annual rainfall is about ten inches.

The subject of the cultivation of the olive is too large to treat satisfactorily in a paper of this character, and I have found some difficulty in compressing it into the space available for the purpose and at the same time bringing out the important features of the plant and the climate required for its cultivation.

Much depends on the manner of the cultivation of the olive, as poor cultivation and lack of knowledge of the proper methods of caring for the trees without exceptionally favorable soil and climate will keep them from fruiting. The common olive in its wild state is a thorny shrub or small tree, does not produce any fruit, and is unattractive in appearance; but by special care and cultivation it has become a tree varying, according to species, at maturity from twenty to forty feet in height, and is by no means destitute of beauty. There are four or five olive trees on the Galveston island which are several years old and have stood some exceptionally severe winters, with frosts. Some of these trees produce fruit of a very good quality, while others, for lack of proper care and cultivation, have never borne. The tree is an evergreen with leathery leaves, which are generally entirely smooth on the upper side and of a whitish gray with minute scales on the under side. This is said to present a pleasing sight when the slightest breeze is passing through olive groves; the effect has been likened to a silver cloud gliding across the landscape. The olive in its cultivated state is beautiful, and among the Greeks a crown of olive twigs was considered the highest honor which could be bestowed upon a person. The olive is by some supposed to have been originally a native of Greece, by others of Syria, and by some of Asia, but the species are now found distributed in nearly all temperate parts of the globe. The touching story of the flight of the dove from Noah's ark, related in Genesis VIII:11, proves the existence of the olive tree in the earliest period of the world's history.

The olive is successfully cultivated in all parts of Spain and Portugal which are not too elevated. It extends over France, south of the mountains of Cevennes; over Italy, south of the Apennines; and over Turkey, south of Haemus. The olive is the staple of Corfu, and it is grown on the northern coast of Africa, in Hong Kong, China, and almost throughout the republic of Chile. It is also stated that with few exceptions the whole basin of the Mediterranean, from the thirty-fifth to the forty-third degree of latitude, is one great belt of olive trees.

General John Bidwell, in an address before the fruit growers' convention of California in 1884, said: "I remember the time when there was no fruit raised in California except at the old missions. Some attempts were made on the ranches to raise a few grapes and perhaps a few pears, but they were invariably failures, so far as I know." It appears from the authorities at hand that few fruits were grown in California prior to the introduction of the Mission olive. Mr. B. M. Lelong, when secretary of the California state board of horticulture, stated that, at the time of the introduction of the Mission olive in California, most of the fruits then consisted of seedling peaches, apples, pears, quinces, pomegranates, and the Mission grape, and that these fruits were so inferior in quality that the "prickly pear" (Tuna opuntia) ranked first in popularity among the people. With these facts before us I can not see why the horticulturists do not try the cultivation of the olive in southern Texas. Its cultivation is carried on successfully in many places along the Pacific coast and is being introduced along the Atlantic coast. It is stated in the report of the Department of Agriculture, 1888, page 35, that "particular attention is, at the present time, being given to the introduction and propagation of the best varieties of the European olive. The cultivation of olive trees and the manufacture of their products have become industries of considerable importance on the Pacific coast, and it is fairly presumed that equal success will follow the introduction of this plant in the southern states, where climatic conditions are favorable for its growth."

Ancient writers upon the olive state that the tree will not thrive remote from the influence of the sea air; and this opinion has been handed down from generation to generation, and is entertained, even at the present day, by men whose opinion on the subject can not be lightly regarded. But Mr. L. A. Bernays, a prominent writer on tropical agriculture, in speaking of this matter says: "The fact, however, that the olive forms a staple product throughout Spain, even in those parts which are so remote from the coast as to be quite beyond the influence of the sea air, seems to set the matter at rest. The idea is probably traditional, and takes its origin in the fact that in the early history of the olive the countries where it was grown were chiefly maritime." This writer believes to some extent that a sea air is beneficial to the plant. The Portuguese oil growers use sea sand in putting out their olive groves, and this may be worth our attention in considering the suitableness of the olive for some parts of Texas: although the oceanic breeze prevails throughout the greater portion of the year, yet a sandy soil is beneficial to the growth of the tree.

The olive tree has been known to stand temperatures as low as 14 degrees and bear that year, and it is believed that the more hardy tree will endure lower temperatures than this and produce fruit, especially if dry weather prevails during the cold spell. A very important feature in the cultivation of the olive is that when injured by cold weather the roots and body of the trees are not affected, and that, if the trunk is properly pruned, sprouts or twigs will grow out and bear fruit when two years old, as it is always the second year's growth of the twig which bears. Some of the olive trees which I have previously mentioned as growing on the Galveston island were there in 1886, when the temperature fell as low as 11 degrees above zero, which is the lowest on record; and during this cold spell the twigs of the trees were killed, but otherwise the plants remained uninjured. The body of a tree which was then growing on West Broadway was pruned, and the new branches which grew out bore fruit in the second year. This tree is still growing there, and I have examined it and am of the opinion that it is a tender olive, which is easily injured by cold, and that a more hardy variety can be secured which will stand the severest winters on the island without being injured to any great extent. The temperature in February this year (1895) fell to about 14 degrees Fahrenheit, and there are trees in Galveston now full of fruit. The above temperature is lower than that ordinarily recorded during the winter over a large area in southern Texas, and such temperatures do not occur on an average oftener than once in twelve years along the immediate coast and over the lower Rio Grande valley.

An olive grove possesses one great advantage over almost every other product which can be grown, that is, its permanency; for when once planted under favorable conditions it is planted practically forever. It is a common saying in Italy, "If you want to leave a lasting inheritance to your children's children, plant an olive." The olive is unlike the peach, apple, mulberry, and other trees, for if long neglected it will revive as soon as the ground about it is again stirred and it receives proper attention, and will respond to the care bestowed upon it by yielding fruit in abundance as it did in its early days, when first cultivated. The tree will commence fruiting at about the second or third year of its growth, and the yield will continue increasing until its fiftieth year or upward; but in its sixth year, if it has been properly cared for, the crop will repay the expense of cultivation, even if other crops are not grown on the ground between the trees; after that period the product is the surest source of wealth.

The olive is said to be a healthy and vigorous plant when cultivated under favorable conditions of soil and climate and is a long-lived tree; it has been known to bear fruit for centuries. At the fair in Paris in 1853 there was an exhibit showing the trunk of a wild olive tree of Algeria, thought to be one thousand years old. In the valley of the cascade of Marmora there is a large plantation of olive trees like (and supposed to be) those mentioned by Pliny as growing there in the first century of the Christian era. In fact, the Saracen olive trees in Sicily are extraordinary for age and height, some of which, says Pasquale, "have produced as high as fifty bushels of olives;" although Prof. Aloi says in some of his writings that "the highest production of the largest olive trees of Sicily never exceeds 264 gallons of olives, and even this quantity is but seldom reached."

It is claimed by some writers on this subject that an acre of olive trees in full bearing will average 750 quarts of olive oil; and, when we consider that it retails in this country at about one dollar a quart flask, it is evident that a big profit is made in the cultivation of this fruit. The United States paid for imported olives in 1884 $127,100, and it is believed that this fruit can be cultivated here successfully and an abundance for home consumption can be grown.

The olive requires a sandy soil, not overly rich, but well drained. It accustoms itself to both dry and wet climates, but clay and mud are unfavorable to it. One writer on this subject states that the olive will thrive and be most prolific in dry, calcareous, schistous, sandy, or rocky situations. However, the horticulturist should consider the wants of the tree. All plant food is comprised principally of three elements—nitrogen, potash and phosphoric acid—and these must be furnished in such quantities as will best promote the growth of the tree and do it in the most economical way. If the soil is supplied with too much nitrogen, it causes a sappy growth of the wood, which puts it in a condition to be easily injured by frost or heat; and this must be avoided in the cultivation of the olive, as it will have a tendency to take on its growth too early in the spring in this climate, which may cause the late frosts to damage the tree to some extent in some years. A greater per cent of potash than both the other named elements combined is found in plants; this element has a tendency to harden the growth of trees, and it may be necessary to use it as a fertilizer in the cultivation of the olive in some soils.

In planting out the olive one should be sure to let the rows run with the drainage of the land where planted, for the trees will not do well in ill-drained situations, and nothing but disappointment can result without loose, permeable, and well-drained land; and the deeper these conditions exist, the better. The roots of the trees run down deep and find all the moisture they need far below the surface. They are cultivated successfully in portions of California without irrigation where the rainfall is less than that over western Texas. It is reported that in the foothills of Santa Barbara County and around San Jose, California, the frequent fogs are found to yield sufficient surface moisture for the olive, and for the olive alone.

In regard to the distance apart for planting the trees, Mr. L. A. Bernays says: "That must be determined partly by variety and partly by aspect. Of late years the propagation of new and highly productive varieties and the adoption of a system of pruning the trees to such limits as will render the gathering of the fruit by hand comparatively easy has enabled cultivators to bring their trees closer together, and thus to economize space and consolidate their operations. Orchards are now planted at distances ranging from sixteen feet up to a maximum of thirty feet, according to variety, the distance being further regulated by the quality of the soil." I would suggest that the trees be planted from twenty to thirty-five feet apart to experiment with, as better fruit can be grown under these conditions; and then small grain crops can be grown for a few years on the intermediate ground without injuring the olive to any extent.

There are several methods of propagation, but I think the best way to secure the plants here is by cuttings, which grow and do well. Suckers, seedling, and grafting all do very well. Then there is a method of propagation by Uovoli. This method is both curious and interesting, states one writer. "The word is Italian and means literally 'little eggs'." These Uovoli or embryo buds are a kind of woody excrescence formed under the growth of the bark on trees, and at the age of ten years and upward of the tree they can be removed, with a piece of bark being left on the Uovoli, and planted like bulbs, in a manner somewhat similar to propagating the potato by eyes; and in due course they become young trees. This method of propagation is not practiced very much except when large trees are to be removed or destroyed in the orchards.

Suckers rise in abundance from the roots of the old trees, and these, transplanted, become trees in their turn; but, as cuttings from the olive take root so readily, this is the most common method of obtaining young trees. To illustrate the case of the propagation of the olive by this latter method I will give a quite interesting story contained in the "Account of the Empire of Morocco," by Mr. Jackson. He mentions a large plantation of olive trees near Messa which struck him as being, to say the least, "very odd in the arrangement of the trees, for they were planted here, there, everywhere, sometimes in large groups, sometimes in small, sometimes singly and again in short rows or angles; order nowhere, eccentricity reigning supreme."

In speaking of this he says that inquiry brought to light the following history: "I learned from the viceroy's aide-de-camp, who attended me, that one of the kings of the dynasty of Saddia, being on his journey to Soudan, encamped here with his army; that the pegs with which the cavalry picketed their horses were cut from the olive trees in the neighborhood, and that, these pegs being left in the ground on account of some sudden cause of the departure of the army, the olive trees in question sprang from them. And the disposition of the trees did exactly resemble the arrangement of cavalry in an encamp-ment."

Cuttings should be taken from the trees in December or January, neatly trimmed, and carefully trenched in loose sandy and shady soil if convenient; and then, about March 1, depend-ing upon the season, they can be planted in permanent sites. In regard to the variety of olives, it may be necessary to try several species before finding the best for this climate and soil. The Mission and Picholine olives, which are cultivated in California, will do well in parts of the Texas coast country. The Redouanou is a species of olive which is grown in France. It is a hardy tree and stands cold well, and I would recommend it for this climate. The Bermillaon, Empeltree, Gordal, Neva-dillo Negro, Recimal, Rostrata, Rubicans, Verdeso, Varal Blanco and Verdego (one of the most hardy of all varieties) are hardy trees and are generally considered excellent bearers. These trees are recommended for warm as well as cool climates and are said to resist frost well. The fruit of the majority of the above-named olives ripens early, but late maturing varieties will prob-ably do well in this climate. Many other species of olives which will probably grow and do well here could be mentioned, but space will not admit of it.

The soil should be frequently stirred for some distance around the trees, especially for the first year. All weeds and grass should be kept down, and if small grain crops are grown on the land the seeds should not be sown closer than from three to four feet of the tree, as this space should be kept clean to furnish nutrition to the olive plant. These cuttings will throw up numerous shoots or sprouts and should be left to grow the first year; and in the following spring, when the ground is warm and sufficiently dry, all sprouts excepting the ones to be preserved should be carefully removed, cutting them off close to the cutting. The top end of the cutting should also be removed by a sharp pruning knife or saw. It is believed that a great deal of time can be saved and better trees can be secured by planting posts, so that the trees can be protected and the trunk can be kept straight. This post will prevent any disturbance of the roots by the winds shaking the tree, and will give them a firmer growth; it should be left until the tree is five or six years old.

We learn from some of the most reliable books published in the French, Spanish and Italian languages on the cultivation of the olive, that it is the habit of the tree to overbear, and that as a consequence it will give but little fruit the year following a heavy crop. In fact, in some olive countries the trees produce fruit only every other year. The cause of these irregular crops is by some believed to be neglect of the proper cultivation of the trees, but others believe that in the year in which they bear the fruit it is allowed to remain on the trees too long and thereby affects the next year's crop. The olive if left to itself will bear only once in two years, but with well-managed plantations annual crops can be secured. This latter statement has been proved by the cultivation of the olive in California. Mr. Davis, who had charge of the San Diego Mission orchard in 1875, said that he had gathered over 150 gallons of olives from the same tree two years in succession, and this suffices to prove that the trees will bear annual crops if well cared for.

Mulching the trees while young will be of great benefit to the growth of the plant, especially during warm and dry weather. The mulch will retain the moisture and keep the surface of the soil cool, which will be beneficial to the tree during the summer. Grass, straw, or any such substance can be used, but one should select something free from seeds, something which will gradually decay and, when dug in, will act as a fertilizer.

The fruit is produced on the twigs of the preceding years, and the time for gathering is the eve of maturity, expecially for making oil. If the fruit is allowed to remain on the tree until it gets ready to fall, it is too ripe for the finest quality of oil, and under these conditions some claim that the quantity of the oil is reduced in the berry by allowing the fruit to become over-ripe. There are different methods of gathering the fruit, but the greater portion of it is picked from the trees by hand. In some places sheets of cloth are put under the trees, and then the fruit is frailed off, but this is injurious to the tree. And, as Mr. B. M. Delong says, "The ancients knew better how to appreciate the olive; they forbade by law the beating of the precious tree of Minerva. So great was their veneration for it that they respected religiously the famous precept which formed a part of their code: 'Do not cut or strike the olive.' "

Olives are used in many ways which are too numerous to mention. Pickled olives are a delicacy on almost any table. In some localities the oil takes the place of butter. The oil is exported into some countries for medicinal purposes, although it is stated by some writers even at the present time that olive oil is adulterated to a great extent, as the supply can not be made to meet the demands. The oil constitutes the great commercial value of the cultivation of the olive tree. The oil obtained from the fruit when first pressed is carefully separated, and is generally known as the "virgin oil." It is of exceptionally fine quality and commands the highest price. It is reported by the writer on tropical agriculture in "Chambers Encyclopaedia" that "it is chiefly from the pericarp that olive oil is obtained, not from the seed, contrary to the general rule of the vegetable kingdom." A fixed quantity of oil is contained in the pericarp, shell, and kernel, and some classify the tree and its fruits with the lilac, the ash, and the privet.

Several opinions prevail in regard to manufacturing olive oil, but as no olives for this purpose are cultivated in the state it is not necessary to dwell upon this part of the question any longer.

Now, I think that the horticulturists of southern Texas, when they bear in mind the longevity of the olive tree, its great productiveness, its manifold uses for food, and the various uses to which its products can be put, should take up the cultivation of this fruit and test its importance and usefulness. You who do not wish to expend what is necessary for the establishment of a large olive grove can plant olive trees just inside the fences of your cultivated fields, and by this means experiment with the trees without risk of loss. But I will say now that, when you put in a few score of trees in this way and discover in a few years that you are able to manufacture oil more than enough for family use, you will require no persuasion to plant on a larger scale and will regret the present lack of confidence in the cultivation of this fruit. Many said a few

years ago that the fruits now grown in Texas could not be cultivated here, and made the statement in good faith; but they
lacked the knowledge of the conditions under which these fruits
thrived.

I am convinced that the olive will thrive in Texas as far
north as the thirtieth, and possibly to the thirty-first parallel
of latitude, and it is believed that, in the course of a few years,
the cultivation of the olive will be one of the leading industries
carried on over the southern portions of the state.   However,
I consider the cultivation of this fruit in southern Texas of
interest to the horticulturists of the northern part of the state,
for that which is beneficial to the people of part of the state
will in time be of benefit to those of the other part.   In fact,
if the horticulturists of the southern portion of the state can
cultivate a fruit which can not be grown in the northern portion, they can afford to do so; then those of the northern portion can cultivate a fruit which is not grown in the southern
portion, and by this method all will be benefited alike and
will not affect the markets of each other's products, and hence
will obtain a better price for their fruits.

Galveston, Texas, June 29, 1895.

SPECIAL ADDRESS ON HURRICANES STRIKING WEST TEXAS COAST

By Joseph L. Cline, B. Sc.; A. M.; Ph. D.

The hurricane that just passed inland on the Texas coast had its origin in the West Indies and moved westward near Cuba and the Florida Keys, after which it apparently took a direct west course near the middle Gulf of Mexico. It remained in the Gulf of Mexico from Tuesday, September 9, to Sunday, September 14, 1919. At one time it began to curve from its west course to a. northerly direction and appeared as though it might move inland over Louisiana; but an area of high pressure formed to the northward that caused it to continue on its westward journey through the Gulf. The hurricanes of the West Indies generally commence forming on a small scale, something like a whirlwind or a thunderstorm, between latitudes 10° and 20° North and are similar to the typhoons of the East Indies, which are so dreaded in portions of Japan. They increase in intensity and become cyclones possessing destructive power. They have a progressive movement across the country, often amounting to only a few miles per hour, while the gyratory, or spiral, character of the winds around their center may amount to 60 or more than 100 miles per hour. Owing to the mobility of water, these hurricanes increase in intensity when moving over water surfaces, which accounts for their destructive force after reaching latitudes 21° to 30° North; but when they pass inland they decrease in intensity and soon lose their destructive force. This is believed to be generally due to the resistance in the pressure of the atmosphere upon coming in contact with the rigid land surfaces. The time which it takes for a hurricane to pass over a given place lying within its path varies from a few hours to a day or more. The most dangerous portion of such hurricanes is forward and to the right of their center in this country, as the winds are usually most violent in this quadrant; however, the highest water may be expected near the eye, or center, of the hurricanes, on account of the inward spiral wind, causing what is occasionally called a "double-wave."

Many people believe such hurricanes to be a result of the equinox, but meteorologists do not concur in the popular belief of equinoxial gales, or storms. It is generally conceded by scientists that changes in the condition of the atmosphere as a result of the approach of the equinox are so slight daily that such storms can hardly be attributed to the equinox. The seasons at which these hurricanes are observed are the late summer and early autumn months; some have occurred in June and July, but they are more frequent in August, September and October. We are taught by scientists that, in these months, the equatorial calms, or doldrums, of the Atlantic migrate farthest north of the equator, and that, in tracing the hurricanes backward along their track, it is found that it is in the calm region of warm, moist air between the trade winds that the West Indian hurricanes have their beginning. Such a region of quiet air is the natural seat of pronounced convectional action. The air in such conditions becomes warm and well moistened by evaporation, and the warm moist air becomes unstable, taking on a gradual convectional overturning; this is believed by some scientists to be the origin, or beginning, of these hurricanes.

Some of the West India hurricanes curve north-northeastward before reaching the Gulf of Mexico and never touch the United States. Many that come into the Gulf curve northward and move inland over Louisiana, Mississippi, Alabama or Florida, and some move inland from the Atlantic Ocean over the South Atlantic States. A few other West India hurricanes have moved inland over the extreme South Texas coast; then crossed the Rio Grande Valley, and dissipated in the mountains of Old Mexico, like the one that passed near Corpus Christi, Texas, last Sunday. This hurricane, which did so much damage on the Texas coast, is believed to be the most severe storm that ever struck west of Indianola, Texas.

Many a vessel and crew have been swept by these hurricanes, and, before the general law concerning the circulation of winds around a storm was known, vessels were often steered into their whirling vortex and lost. Captains who know the wind circulation generally go out of their way and elude such storms.

As to the frequency of West India hurricanes, it may be said that the annual number seldom exceeds six or eight, and only a few of these prove to be very destructive; generally about one a year. From 1800 to within the last few years there was, on an average, one in each seven years that reached some portion of the Gulf coast with a force so marked as to leave a path of destruction in its wake.

The United States Government has established meteorological stations in the West Indies for the purpose of reporting hurricanes. Reports are also received from vessels equipped with wireless apparatus that encounter these storms. In this way the United States Weather Bureau is furnished weather information from which warnings of the approach of hurricanes are issued. These warnings enable people to somewhat protect property and to move to places of safety; and, when people heed the warnings, the loss of life and property is reduced to a minimum. Many vessels remained in places of safety during the recent storm as a result of warnings, and, no doubt, thousands of lives were saved by the timely warnings issued by the U. S. Weather Bureau; with proper precautionary measures and action, many more lives would have been saved. It is better to prepare for a storm when forecasted, even though the hurricane does not come, than to be caught unaware, and remain in the path of a storm and lose your life.

The above article was written at request of the Dallas *Morning News* and the *Times Herald,* and given to the press for publication, September 16, 1919. This was after Corpus Christi, Texas, had been struck by two severe hurricanes: one on Friday, August 18, 1916, and the other on Sunday, September 14, 1919. Both of these hurricanes did considerable damage to property in the vicinity of Corpus Christi. There was no loss of life during the storm of 1916, while the official report as to loss of life in the hurricane of 1919 was placed at 357.

While I was stationed at Corpus Christi, Texas, as Official in Charge, U. S. Weather Bureau Office, there was another hurricane, which almost destroyed Port Aransas, Texas, and flooded north portions of Corpus Christi; but no lives were lost then, as I had the citizens leave Tarpon Island and go to the main land by boat before the storm struck there. I also had most of the people at Corpus Christi moved from the lowlands there that were overflowed during the storm, which accounts for no lives being lost during that hurricane.

After the 1919 hurricane that drowned so many people at Corpus Christi, Mr. Eli Merriman, a prominent Corpus

Christi official and for many years editor of the Corpus Christi *Caller,* leading newspaper of that city, visited me at Dallas, and, while there, said, "If you had only been at Corpus, you would again have had the people move from the lowlands to the Bluff, and there would have been no loss of life."

If weather forecasters had read the above article on hurricanes, showing what caused the hurricane of September 9 to September 14, 1919, to move west in the Gulf of Mexico to the west Texas coast, they might have not frightened so many people along the middle and west Gulf coasts during the hurricane that played with them in the Gulf of Mexico for several days in September, 1943. It appears that a high pressure area to the north of the Gulf of Mexico kept the storm from coming inland from the Gulf sooner than it did. A high pressure area to the north caused the hurricane of 1900 to change its northeastward course just west of Florida, move west in the Gulf of Mexico, and destroy half the residence portion of Galveston, Texas. Forecasters should always remember that storms generally take the course in which they meet with least resistance. That is why tornadoes follow valleys, as it is more difficult for them to climb the resisting hills and mountains.

COMPARISON OF DROUTH OF 1925 WITH OTHER DRY YEARS

By Joseph L. Cline

(Weather Bureau Office, Dallas, Texas, October 20, 1925.)

There are times, in many sections of the country, when growing crops would be improved by more rainfall, and such conditions occur in this locality, especially after the middle of June. But crops in this vicinity, particularly cotton, have often been damaged by too much rain during April, May, and first part of June, and occasionally by excessive rains later in the season. Some statisticians assert that heavy rains generally result in more damage to the cotton crop in Texas than drouths. So far as known, however, there has never been a complete crop failure in this part of Texas.

The precipitation record from 1874 to date shows many drouthy periods of short duration at Dallas, Texas, and two extended, severe drouths that became serious. One of these occurred in 1909-10, and the other in 1925.

The drouth of 1909-10 was apparently the most severe, longest, and most damaging dry period that ever occurred in this locality. This drouth commenced near the close of 1908, and prevailed until about February 8, 1911. There were a few good local rains, somewhat relieving this drouth, but rainfall was generally insufficient for growing crops, and for run-off to fill lakes and reservoirs. Total precipitation at Dallas, Texas, from December, 1908, to November, 1909, inclusive, was 15.58 inches, the smallest consecutive 12-months precipitation of record. The annual rainfall in the year 1909 was 17.98 inches, and only 23.84 inches fell in 1910, making these the driest consecutive years since the records have been kept.

Crops during this severe drouth were not failures, but yields were considerably reduced. It is believed the yield of cotton in pounds per acre in 1909 was the lowest of record, as a direct result of dry weather, the yield averaging only about 125 pounds per acre for Texas. Yield per acre for the State has been less in a few other years, when poorer crops were apparently due to a combination of causes.

At time of this long drouth the City of Dallas had but two reservoirs for impounding water—one at Record Crossing, and the other at Bachman's; but water was also obtained for city use from surface and artesian wells. The reservoirs became dry, and pumps at City Water Works were stopped in September, 1910, and were not started again until some time in February, 1911. During this interim, water for household and culinary purposes was delivered in tanks and wagons to residences in Dallas, Texas. Oak Cliff, Texas, which is a part of Dallas that is located on the west side of Trinity River, had artesian wells from which water was obtained throughout the drouth, and citizens of Oak Cliff still have their artesian water.

The drouth of 1925 commenced in 1924, and total precipitation at Dallas, Texas, from November 9, 1924 to April 24, 1925, inclusive, was 6.20 inches. There was a period of good rains, amounting to 5.60 inches, from April 25 to May 10, 1925, which somewhat relieved the drouth, but rainfall was not sufficient to impound much water in ponds, lakes and reservoirs. These rains were followed by another dry period, from May 11 to September 10, 1925, inclusive, when total rainfall was 6.99 inches, with amounts too small to measure from May 11 to June 5, both dates inclusive. But rains since September 10, 1925, have completely relieved the drouthy conditions.

Crops during the year 1925 were badly damaged by the drouth. Very few vegetables withstood the dry period during May, June, and July. Crops this year range from very poor to very good, with condition depending on intensity of showers, which have been scattered and insufficient for general farming interests. Water for livestock and other purposes became scarce in most sections. Many farmers had to haul water for several miles. Nearly all lakes and reservoirs went dry. Prior to relief from this drouth, the City of Dallas had but one reservoir from which water could be obtained. The lowest amount of available water for use by the City of Dallas at any time during this drouth was estimated at 3,169,094,236 gallons, in White Rock reservoir, April, 1925. White Rock reservoir was constructed immediately after the drouth of 1909-10, and had it not been for this lake the City of Dallas would probably have had to haul water again for household and culinary purposes.

While the showers and local rains of 1925 were not sufficient for corn, vegetables, pastures, and some other growing crops when rain was most needed, they did keep cotton growing during the greater portion of the drouth. It is now apparent that the yield of cotton, which is the staple crop of this section, will be more per acre in 1925 than the yield was in 1909, and possibly, greater than the yield in several other years.

Since the drouth of 1909-10, the City of Dallas has constructed dams for impounding water at California Crossing and Carrollton on Elm Fork of the Trinity River, and also at White Rock. And now one of the largest reservoirs of the country is being constructed at Garza, Texas. When the Garza dam is completed and proper precautionary measures have been taken, the City of Dallas should never experience another water shortage.

Dry periods, with continuous sunshine and few or no clouds, are conducive to hot weather. By perusing all records of the U. S. Weather Bureau, and the files of records kept by Mr. G. A. Eisenlohr, Co-operative Observer, U. S. Weather Bureau, Dallas, Texas, for many years, we find that the highest extreme maximum temperature at Dallas, Texas, occurred during the drouth of 1909-10. According to Mr. Eisenlohr's records the maximum temperature, Fahrenheit, at Dallas, Texas, on August 17, 1909, was 107°. On August 18 it was 112°. On August 19 it was 115°. And on August 20 it was 106°. This shows a mean maximum temperature for the four days in August, 1909, of 110 degrees at Dallas, Texas, which is the heat record for this city. I was told by a reliable man that two of the most prominent men in this city fried an egg on the sidewalk on the west side of Akard Street, near Commerce Street, on the afternoon of August 19, 1909, when the temperature was 115 degrees.

PRECIPITATION AND DEPARTURE FROM THE NORMAL FOR TEXAS 1891 TO 1917, INCLUSIVE

There is a demand for records of precipitation, because a person conversant with crop production, who knows the prevailing temperatures, character of soil, and acreage planted, can consider the amount of precipitation that falls over the agricultural portions of a country and foretell with some degree of accuracy the probable yield of farm products.

Precipitation data used by the U. S. Weather Bureau include rain, sleet, hail, and snow, and these data, as a rule, define, or outline, the agricultural portions of any State. Different opinions prevail in regard to the question of what constitutes an arid region. This question has been discussed by many able men, some claiming that 20 inches of rain per annum is necessary for successful agriculture. The quantity of precipitation necessary for successful agricultural interests depends considerably on the temperature and the character of the soil, the rapidity with which evaporation takes place in the surface soil and the surrounding air, the distribution of the rainfall through the various months, and the kind of crops, as some products require more water than others. When the precipitation in Texas during the winter months has averaged 2.50 to 3.50 inches per month, it is generally considered that there is a good season in the ground as far as cotton is concerned, and that the plant, with such conditions of the soil, will develop a normal growth of roots at the outset and will be able to withstand considerable drouth and occasional showers, during the growing season, insuring a fair crop of cotton. But if the monthly rainfall during the winter months is much less than 2.50 inches, the plant will not develop normal growth of roots and will then require regular rains at short intervals during the growing and fruiting season to make a good yield. With the cultivation of maize it is somewhat different, as this crop, owing to numerous surface or shallow roots, requires good rains at uniform intervals during the growing season to insure a good yield. Drouthy conditions at the time of tasseling and silking will always materially reduce the yield of maize. The precipitation in March and April and the early part of May plays the most important part in the cultivation of oats in Texas. Wheat cultivation is carried on most successfully where the precipitation is fairly distributed from the time the grain is sown until ready for harvesting. Good crops of wheat have been grown in the Dakotas with an annual rainfall of about 15 inches.

(For more complete information on this subject see paper entitled "Crop Production in Texas Compared with Temperature and Precipitation Departures, for Eight Years", Special Bulletin No. 2, Texas Weather Service, by present author.)

The annual isohyetals, or lines of equal rainfall for the year, traverse Texas in a southerly and northerly direction, nearly parallel with the meridians of longitude. In the extreme eastern portion of the State the annual normal precipitation is slightly above 45 inches, and it decreases to the west at the rate of about 2 inches in 30 miles until the extreme western portion of Texas is reached, where the average annual rainfall is slightly less than 10 inches. The average annual or normal precipitation in Texas for the twenty-seven years under consideration is 29.66 inches, and the area where the local annual normal and the average annual normal for the State agree lies between longitude 97° and 98° West. The greatest average annual rainfall in Texas, as shown by the table herewith appended was 42.17 inches in 1900, and the smallest annual average was 16.21 inches in 1917. There was a marked deficiency in precipitation in 1917, being 4.26 inches greater than the deficiency in the previous driest year, 1893. On an average for the State, April and May are the months with the greatest rainfall, and January and February are the months with the smallest precipitation; but this is not the case locally throughout the State, as the greatest monthly precipitation falls in September over the extreme southern portions of Texas.

There were only two months in the twenty-seven years, as shown in the table, when the average precipitation for the State was the same as the average State normal; these months were October, 1903, and November, 1908. The greatest monthly deficiency for the State was 2.23 inches in August, 1902, and the greatest monthly excess in precipitation for the State was 4.39 inches in November, 1902. The greatest average monthly rainfall for the State was 7.68 inches in May, 1914, and the next greatest was 7.07 inches in June, 1899. The smallest average monthly precipitation for the State was .09 inch in February, 1916; the next smallest monthly average was .17 inch in November, 1903, and the next smallest was .18 inch in December, 1917. The longest and most severe drouth in Texas was prevailing at the close of the year 1917, there having been a deficiency in precipitation for the State

(Appendage to foregoing article)

The following Table shows the Average precipitation and the Departure from the Normal by Months and Years for Texas, 1891 to 1917, inclusive.
(in inches)

	Jan.	Feb.	Mch.	Apr.	May	June	July	Aug.	Sept.	Oct.	Nov.	Dec.	Year
1891; Average	5.05	1.08	1.57	4.36	2.38	2.66	2.41	1.64	2.83	0.56	1.49	4.42	30.45
Departure	+3.51	−0.64	−0.37	+1.30	−1.30	−0.24	−0.36	−0.89	+0.14	−1.89	−0.69	+2.22	+0.79
1892; Average	1.24	1.11	2.25	1.38	3.24	3.21	1.96	3.88	1.40	4.08	2.32	3.33	29.40
Departure	−0.30	−0.61	+0.31	−1.68	−0.44	+0.31	−0.81	+1.35	−1.29	+1.63	+0.14	+1.13	−0.26
1893; Average	0.89	1.11	1.41	1.78	3.65	2.62	0.96	2.35	1.59	0.33	2.92	0.86	20.47
Departure	−0.65	−0.61	−0.53	−1.28	−0.03	−0.28	−1.81	−0.18	−1.10	−2.12	+0.74	−1.34	−9.19
1894; Average	1.55	1.71	2.69	3.51	3.39	2.63	2.10	5.24	2.72	0.94	0.40	0.77	27.65
Departure	+0.01	−0.01	+0.75	+0.45	−0.29	−0.27	−0.67	+2.71	+0.03	−1.51	−1.78	−1.43	−2.01
1895; Average	1.51	2.03	1.48	1.72	6.05	5.29	3.20	2.23	1.65	2.50	3.35	1.91	32.92
Departure	−0.03	+0.31	−0.46	−1.34	+2.37	+2.39	+0.43	−0.30	−1.04	+0.05	+1.17	−0.29	+3.26
1896; Average	3.14	2.84	1.42	1.86	1.29	1.04	2.64	1.27	4.57	4.26	1.23	1.85	27.41
Departure	+1.60	+1.12	−0.52	−1.20	−2.39	−1.86	−0.13	−1.26	+1.88	+1.81	−0.95	−0.35	−2.25
1897; Average	2.50	0.41	3.57	1.93	3.93	3.06	1.23	2.46	2.44	2.90	0.52	2.37	27.32
Departure	+0.96	−1.31	+1.63	−1.13	+0.25	+0.16	−1.54	−0.07	−0.25	+0.45	−1.66	+0.17	−2.34
1898; Average	1.91	1.86	2.10	2.45	2.65	5.33	2.20	2.62	1.88	1.19	2.11	2.13	28.43
Departure	+0.37	+0.14	+0.16	−0.61	−1.03	+2.43	−0.57	+0.09	−0.81	−1.26	−0.07	−0.07	−1.23
1899; Average	2.15	0.84	0.47	2.86	2.58	7.07	2.58	0.94	1.61	3.46	2.72	1.42	28.70
Departure	+0.61	−0.88	−1.47	−0.20	−1.10	+4.17	−0.19	−1.59	−1.08	+1.01	+0.54	−0.78	−0.96
1900; Average	2.80	1.20	3.61	6.66	4.99	2.11	5.52	3.73	5.20	3.30	1.79	1.26	42.17
Departure	+1.26	−0.52	+1.67	+3.60	+1.31	−0.79	+2.75	+1.20	+2.51	+0.85	−0.39	−0.94	+12.51
1901; Average	0.60	1.78	1.43	1.97	3.42	1.27	2.46	1.55	3.38	1.69	1.63	1.05	22.23
Departure	−0.94	+0.06	−0.51	−1.09	−0.26	−1.63	−0.31	−0.98	+0.69	−0.76	−0.55	−1.15	−7.43
1902; Average	0.89	1.05	1.81	2.08	3.93	1.96	5.84	0.30	5.02	2.46	6.57	2.01	33.92
Departure	−0.65	−0.67	−0.13	−0.98	+0.25	−0.94	+3.07	−2.23	+2.33	+0.01	+4.39	−0.19	+4.26
1903; Average	2.33	5.66	3.21	1.03	2.29	4.10	5.81	2.18	2.52	2.45	0.17	1.28	33.03
Departure	+0.79	+3.94	+1.27	−2.03	−1.39	+1.20	+3.04	−0.35	−0.17	+0.00	−2.01	−0.92	+3.37

	Jan.	Feb.	Mch.	Apr.	May	June	July	Aug.	Sept.	Oct.	Nov.	Dec.	Year
1904; Average	0.71	1.56	1.05	2.98	4.56	4.28	2.70	2.25	3.99	2.89	0.99	2.06	30.02
Departure	-0.83	-0.16	-0.89	-0.08	+0.88	+1.38	-0.07	-0.28	+1.30	-0.44	-1.19	-0.14	+0.36
1905; Average	1.63	2.61	4.29	6.32	4.82	4.64	4.06	1.20	2.31	2.61	3.62	3.62	41.73
Departure	+0.09	+0.89	+2.35	+3.26	+1.14	+1.74	+1.29	-1.33	-0.38	+0.16	+1.44	+1.42	+12.07
1906; Average	1.15	1.86	1.72	2.67	2.98	2.71	4.71	3.54	3.47	2.58	2.01	2.11	31.51
Departure	-0.39	+0.14	-0.22	-0.39	-0.70	-0.19	+1.94	+1.01	+0.78	+0.13	-0.17	-0.09	+1.85
1907; Average	1.04	1.25	1.64	2.42	6.73	1.71	2.85	1.81	1.66	5.35	5.40	2.00	33.86
Departure	-0.50	-0.47	-0.30	-0.64	+3.05	-1.19	+0.08	-0.72	-1.03	+2.90	+3.22	-0.20	+4.20
1908; Average	1.06	2.65	1.65	5.08	5.69	2.48	2.90	3.00	3.28	1.79	2.18	1.15	32.91
Departure	0.48	0.93	0.29	2.01	2.01	-0.42	+0.13	+0.47	+0.59	-0.66	+0.00	-1.05	+3.25
1909; Average	0.15	0.90	1.08	1.55	3.06	3.37	2.40	2.17	1.03	2.47	2.72	2.55	23.45
Departure	-1.39	-0.82	-0.86	-1.51	-0.62	+0.47	-0.37	-0.36	-1.66	+0.02	+0.54	+0.35	-6.21
1910; Average	0.85	1.52	1.55	2.59	3.91	1.90	1.37	1.25	1.80	1.73	0.73	2.26	21.46
Departure	-0.69	-0.20	-0.39	-0.47	+0.23	-1.00	-1.40	-1.28	-0.89	-0.72	-1.45	+0.06	-8.20
1911; Average	0.37	2.77	2.19	4.88	2.13	0.88	3.71	2.07	1.61	2.09	1.51	4.92	29.13
Departure	-1.17	+1.05	0.25	+1.82	-1.55	-2.02	+0.94	-0.46	-1.08	-0.36	-0.67	+2.72	-0.53
1912; Average	0.51	2.13	2.75	2.87	2.28	3.71	1.20	2.49	1.52	2.79	1.12	2.75	26.12
Departure	-1.03	+0.41	+0.81	-0.19	-1.40	+0.81	-1.57	-0.04	-1.17	+0.34	-1.06	+0.55	-3.54
1913; Average	1.60	2.03	1.69	2.02	2.55	3.61	1.29	1.26	6.63	4.35	3.99	5.03	36.05
Departure	+0.06	+0.31	-0.25	-1.04	-1.13	+0.71	-1.48	-1.27	+3.94	+1.90	+1.81	+2.83	+6.39
1914; Average	0.35	1.53	2.45	4.28	7.68	1.47	1.51	6.37	1.46	3.46	3.78	3.54	37.88
Departure	-1.19	-0.19	+0.51	+1.22	+4.00	-1.43	-1.26	+3.84	-1.23	+1.01	+1.60	+1.34	+8.22
1915; Average	1.97	1.89	1.83	5.82	2.47	2.24	2.07	6.05	3.17	1.54	1.01	1.95	32.01
Departure	+0.43	+0.17	-0.11	+2.76	-1.21	-0.66	-0.70	+3.52	+0.48	-0.91	-1.17	+0.25	+2.35
1916; Average	2.68	0.09	0.64	3.44	3.80	2.17	2.71	2.84	1.86	2.07	1.60	0.69	24.59
Departure	+1.14	+0.09	-1.30	+0.38	+0.12	-0.73	-0.06	+0.31	-0.83	-0.38	-0.58	-1.51	-5.07
1917; Average	1.05	0.95	0.94	2.17	2.76	0.80	2.27	1.73	1.99	0.33	1.04	0.18	16.21
Departure	-0.49	-0.77	-1.00	-0.89	-0.92	-2.10	-0.50	-0.80	-0.70	-2.12	-1.14	-2.02	-13.45
Normal	1.54	1.72	1.94	3.06	3.68	2.90	2.77	2.53	2.69	2.45	2.18	2.20	29.66

Above from Climatological Data, Texas Section.

during each of the preceding sixteen months. This drouth was severe and disastrous for farming and live stock interests, especially in the western half of Texas.

The variability of rainfall plays an important part in agricultural and other interests. The number of rainy days in Texas varies in the same months over the different portions of the State, and the rainfall distribution by days is not the same in every year. On a general average, or with normal conditions, rain may be expected, or anticipated, over the Panhandle and Llano Estacado about once in eight days from October to February and about once in every five or six days during the remainder of the year. Over the southern and eastern portions of the State, rainy days are more frequent, and rain may be looked for on an average every four or five days, except from June to January, inclusive, when the number of rainy days is more frequent, especially along the east coast.

Periods of dry and wet weather of sufficient intensity and duration to materially affect crops occasionally occur, especially over the western half of Texas. However, in traversing the State we find agricultural land, not yet under cultivation, where the rainfall is abundant for agricultural purposes, and as a rule the amount that falls is fairly well distributed throughout the year. Periods of dry and wet weather may be expected in the future, particularly over the western sections of the State. Such conditions are not rare, as they prevail in other countries. It is believed that the seven fat years and the seven lean years, or the seven years of plenty and the seven years of famine, in Egypt, foretold by Joseph as recorded in sacred history (Genesis, XLI) as the interpretation of King Pharaoh's dream, represented cycles, or periods, of seven years of rain with excellent crops and seven years of drouth with poor crops; however, if so, such cycles are not so marked in this country as they were in Egypt.

Owing to the kind of crops grown and the improved methods of cultivation introduced through the U. S. Department of Agriculture, the drouthy periods in the semiarid regions of the west are not now so noticeable as they were in the past, when crops grown and methods of cultivation practiced required more moisture. This improvement in crop production as a result of the change has caused some people to assert that the rainfall has increased, but the records do not show such to be the case. Where continuous records have been kept they show cycles, or periods, of excess and deficiency in precipitation in recent years, just as in olden times. There are periods of dry and wet weather everywhere, and there will likely be as long as time lasts; but, where the rainfall is sufficient and all other climatic conditions favorable, land can be made to yield bountiful crops. Soil can be changed artificially and made productive, but an adverse climate will probably remain so forever.

(Appendage to foregoing article)

COMPARISON OF WINTER AND SPRING PRECIPITATION IN RELATION TO ACREAGE AND YIELD OF COTTON IN TEXAS

Winter of	Precipitation, in Inches							Cotton, total acreage	Yield in running bales
	Dec.	Jan.	Feb.	Mch.	Apr.	May	Total		
1892-93 ..	3.33	0.89	1.11	1.41	1.78	3.65	12.17	4,153,760	1,997,000
1893-94 ..	0.86	1.55	1.71	2.69	3.51	3.39	13.71	6,854,621	3,140,392
1894-95 ..	0.77	1.51	2.03	1.48	1.72	6.05	13.56	5,826,428	1,905,337
1895-96 ..	1.91	3.14	2.84	1.42	1.86	1.29	12.46	6,758,656	2,122,701
1896-97 ..	1.85	2.50	0.41	3.57	1.93	3.93	14.19	7,164,175	2,822,408
1897-98 ..	2.37	1.91	1.86	2.10	2.45	2.65	13.34	6,991,904	3,363,109
1898-99 ..	2.13	2.15	0.84	0.47	2.86	2.58	11.03	6,960,367	2,525,324
1899-00 ..	1.42	2.80	1.20	3.61	6.66	4.99	20.68	7,178,915	3,329,015
1900-01 ..	1.26	0.60	1.78	1.43	1.97	3.42	10.46	7,656,312	2,447,834
1901-02 ..	1.05	0.89	1.05	1.81	2.08	3.93	10.81	7,640,531	2,427,994
1902-03 ..	2.01	2.33	5.66	3.21	1.03	2.29	16.53	7,801,578	2,406,146
1903-04 ..	1.28	0.71	1.56	1.05	2.98	4.56	12.14	8,355,491	3,062,203
1904-05 ..	2.06	1.63	2.61	4.29	6.32	4.82	21.73	6,945,501	2,432,718
1905-06 ..	3.62	1.15	1.86	1.72	2.67	2.98	14.00	8,894,000	3,957,619
1906-07 ..	2.11	1.04	1.25	1.64	2.42	6.73	15.19	9,156,000	2,208,021
1907-08 ..	2.00	1.06	2.65	1.65	5.08	5.69	18.13	9,316,000	3,627,350
1908-09 ..	1.15	0.15	0.90	1.08	1.55	3.06	7.89	9,930,000	2,469,331
1909-10 ..	2.55	0.85	1.52	1.55	2.59	3.91	12.97	10,060,000	2,949,968
1910-11 ..	2.26	0.37	2.77	2.19	4.88	2.13	14.60	10,943,000	4,107,152
1911-12 ..	4.92	0.51	2.13	2.75	2.87	2.28	15.46	11,338,000	4,645,309
1912-13 ..	2.75	1.60	2.03	1.69	2.02	2.55	12.64	12,597,000	3,773,024
1913-14 ..	5.03	0.35	1.53	2.45	4.28	7.68	21.32	11,931,000	4,390,200
1914-15 ..	3.54	1.97	1.89	1.83	5.82	2.47	17.52	10,510,000	3,068,852
1915-16 ..	1.95	2.68	0.09	0.64	3.44	3.80	12.60	11,400,000	3,562,789
1916-17 ..	0.69	1.05	0.95	0.94	2.17	2.76	8.56	11,640,000	3,115,000*
1917-18 ..	0.18	0.82	1.03	1.35					

*Estimate of U. S. Department of Agriculture in 500 pound bales.

Final estimate by ginners of bales ginned and to be ginned, March, 1918, was 3,040,268 running bales.

(Acreage and yield of cotton used in this table were taken from U. S. Department of Commerce, Bureau of Census, Bulletin 135, "Cotton Production and Distribution," Season 1916-17).

PROTECTION OF CABBAGE AND OTHER VEGE-TABLES IN SOUTHERN TEXAS, FROM KILLING FROSTS AND FREEZING TEMPERATURES, BY IRRIGATION

By JOSEPH L. CLINE, B.SC., A.M.; PH.D.

The cultivation of vegetables for the winter and early spring markets has been carried on over southern Texas to some extent for many years, but, in the last ten years, since large irrigation plants have been put into operation, this industry has been extended until many farmers devote their entire time to truck raising. Occasionally, in severe winters, vegetables that are not protected from killing frosts and freezing temperatures are badly damaged, or destroyed.

Many methods of protecting crops from frost and injurious temperatures have been tried over southern Texas. Some methods, used with success elsewhere, have proved too expensive in most sections of Texas. Smudging by pot-fires, so highly praised in other sections of the United States and some foreign countries, is very expensive, and has not proved a success in portions of southern Texas, because the brisk to high winds that generally accompany cold waves and freezing temperatures carry the smoke and heat away from the crops; however, this method is very beneficial in calm weather.

On account of the prevailing local conditions, covering with hay or cloth and flooding the land with water where possible have proven to be the most successful and least expensive method of protecting small crops in southern Texas from frost or injurious temperatures.

Frost never forms unless condensation of the aqueous vapor in the atmosphere takes place with temperature at, or below, the freezing point. Plants lose their heat principally by radiation and convection, and this takes place more rapidly in some localities than others, depending somewhat upon the character and condition of the soil, the topography of the country, and the degree of cloudiness. Any method of preventing the radiation and convection of heat from plants during unusually cold weather will prove beneficial in protecting crops. The spraying of plants and trees with a fine spray of water on a frosty morning before sunrise is beneficial, but care must be taken, as too large a spray drop will damage some buds by quick thawing.

The water is absorbed by the cells of the frozen plants and buds of the trees as they thaw, often preventing the bursting of the cells and disorganization of the plant tissues, so that damage from the freeze is greatly reduced.

During the winter of 1904 and 1905 I had an excellent winter garden in my yard, and observed the effects of a severe freeze, especially on cabbage, in the vicinity of Corpus Christi, Texas. The cabbage heads were about eight inches in diameter when a cold wave with a minimum temperature of 18 degrees, Fahrenheit, was experienced. The heads were frozen through, there being ice at the center. The sky remained cloudy during the cold wave; and, as the temperature rose above freezing, a light rain commenced falling. The plants thawed out slowly, and, where earth was thrown up so as to cover the stalk, the cabbage almost fully recovered from the effects of the freeze. Where the stalk was not hilled or covered with dirt, it became diseased in the center and soon decayed, withered, and fell, making it necessary to gather these plants for use immediately, before the disintegration from the stalk entered into the cabbage head. These cabbages were large enough for the market, and were marketed. Cabbage plants that had earth around the stalks continued to grow and in a short time showed practically no effects of the freeze.

At other times, when temperatures of 22 and 28 degrees, Fahrenheit, were experienced with a clear sky, it was observed that, soon after the sun commenced shining and temperature rose above freezing, cabbages and other vegetables were damaged and small plants occasionally killed; but when it rained as the temperature rose to freezing, or above, the damage to truck crops, if any, was generally slight.

When irrigation was put into operation, the truck gardeners near Corpus Christi, Texas, who were prepared to irrigate, kept closely in touch with me, and were always advised to flood their fields when killing frosts or freezing temperatures were expected. A number of truck growers made arrangements to get my forecasts over long-distance telephone at their expense when a freeze was forecasted. They depended upon advice of the Weather Bureau official, who telephoned the warnings, regarding the necessity of flooding their fields. They always observed from actual experience that, when cabbage and other hardy vegetables were flooded with water during periods of freezing temperature, their crops, though sometimes damaged, could generally be saved during the coldest weather experienced in that section of the country. Even when ice formed around the plants, especially cabbage, they appeared to thaw gradually. Plant cells were generally left in normal condition, and crops would continue to grow after the plants and cabbage heads had been frozen.

The following table shows the monthly and annual minimum, or lowest temperatures in degrees (Fahrenheit) at Corpus Christi, Texas, since the station was established, February 1, 1887 to 1913, inclusive:

Year	Jan.	Feb.	Mar.	Apr.	May	June	July	Aug.	Sep.	Oct.	Nov.	Dec.	Ann.
1887	___	33	46	46	57	70	72	72	59	49	33	24	___
1888	16	43	41	57	44	66	73	71	63	50	39	37	16
1889	34	42	45	58	56	69	74	70	56	54	40	46	34
1890	32	30	28	50	58	65	70	74	55	50	42	35	28
1891	33	34	37	46	64	64	70	65	66	51	34	36	33
1892	25	48	31	49	60	64	72	71	65	45	42	27	25
1893	34	33	41	56	57	70	73	69	70	53	40	36	33
1894	24	29	38	58	63	64	70	70	67	42	42	26	24
1895	32	16	38	51	58	70	76	73	62	53	38	28	16
1896	34	39	42	53	65	68	72	70	58	56	30	32	30
1897	22	32	47	52	60	65	72	73	58	55	43	29	22
1898	36	41	40	51	58	64	72	74	69	47	38	28	28
1899	28	11	42	44	66	71	75	75	65	55	41	36	11
1900	29	29	41	47	61	70	72	72	75	54	38	38	29
1901	32	33	42	52	60	67	74	74	60	62	48	20	20
1902	28	35	44	53	63	72	76	73	61	59	41	36	28
1903	35	27	42	52	51	59	68	70	54	50	37	39	27
1904	29	32	38	50	61	68	70	73	70	52	37	33	29
1905	26	18	48	49	63	70	65	73	70	48	46	32	18
1906	30	30	37	53	58	68	72	71	68	52	33	36	30
1907	36	38	48	47	47	65	71	73	67	61	37	44	36
1908	35	38	48	48	53	74	68	70	53	48	39	40	35
1909	24	27	41	48	56	69	75	73	54	53	46	30	24
1910	30	26	48	54	61	68	73	73	70	48	48	44	26
1911	21	37	45	55	57	72	71	73	72	47	29	35	21
1912	22	25	40	53	60	65	74	75	61	54	39	36	22
1913	27	35	37	48	63	71	72	74	59	45	46	41	27
Lwst	16	11	28	44	44	59	65	65	53	42	29	20	11

Another advantage resulting from the protection of vegetables by flooding in southern Texas is that the earth is always warm prior to the approach of cold waves; hence the water radiates heat slowly, preventing the loss of heat by rapid radiation, and as a result air surrounding plants that are flooded is not quite so cold as in fields which are not flooded with water.

Cold waves over southern Texas rarely last more than one or two days. Owing to the short duration of freezing temperatures, cabbage and other hardy vegetables, so far, have not been damaged by the water remaining on the fields where drainage is well provided. Tender plants when left under water several days will not recover from the effects of being flooded, and hence fields should never be flooded until near the approach of injurious temperatures. As soon as the temperature rises above freezing, fields should be drained, so as to prevent damage to plants from being under water too long. Cabbage and other garden truck, where raised in winter months, should be cultivated so that the stalks will be covered with dirt if possible. This makes a ridge or hill around plants, protecting them, to some extent, from the cold. Such cultivation is an aid to quick drainage and recovery from the effects of flooding, as the first soil to be drained is that which immediately surrounds the plants.

When results obtained by flooding crops through freezing weather are compared with the lowest temperatures experienced, the value of protection of crops by irrigation can be ascertained. To enable such a comparison to be made, tables showing lowest

The following table gives the monthly and annual minimum, or lowest temperature in degrees (Fahrenheit) at Fort Brown or Brownsville, Texas, since November 1, 1892 to 1913, inclusive, except during months when no records were kept:

Year	Jan.	Feb.	Mar.	Apr.	May	June	July	Aug.	Sep.	Oct.	Nov.	Dec.	Ann.
1892	----	----	----	----	----	----	----	----	----	----	42	29	----
1893	27	33	42	----	50	62	70	65	67	52	44	33	----
1894	31	27	39	57	64	64	63	69	66	44	46	27	27
1895	32	22	39	48	41	59	57	63	69	56	40	32	22
1896	38	35	40	45	67	66	65	63	51	56	30	----	----
1897	----	----	----	----	----	----	----	67	59	50	43	30	----
1898	----	----	----	----	----	----	----	----	----	----	----	----	----
1899	32	12	45	46	69	67	71	73	60	38	----	----	12
1900	----	27	40	47	64	71	65	71	63	48	37	25	----
1901	----	----	----	----	----	60	----	68	58	53	----	----	----
1902	----	29	40	52	66	70	70	72	63	56	38	35	----
1903	37	26	38	37	51	59	73	73	64	50	40	40	26
1904	32	36	41	51	58	68	69	67	71	50	41	39	32
1905	30	22	48	54	63	68	68	72	68	52	51	33	22
1906	30	32	40	58	61	69	70	72	----	----	----	----	----
1907	----	----	----	----	----	----	70	68	59	36	40	----	----
1908	35	35	46	49	59	72	68	69	58	46	40	38	35
1909	28	29	40	46	61	67	72	71	51	53	54	33	28
1910	30	32	46	46	58	64	71	70	69	44	42	37	30
1911	21	38	49	57	58	68	70	69	71	44	27	34	21
1912	24	27	40	52	56	64	71	70	63	53	39	34	24
1913	30	37	33	44	55	65	69	70	56	45	44	34	30
Low	21	12	33	37	41	59	57	63	51	38	27	25	12

temperatures over southern Texas and remarks of truck growers who saved their crops by protection are given in the accompanying pages.

Following is the statement of Mr. Charles E. Coleman, of Corpus Christi, Texas, one of the leading vegetable men and heaviest shippers of produce by express in southwest Texas, relative to protection of cabbage from freezing temperatures by flooding. Mr. Coleman says:

"During the winter of 1910 and 1911, I purchased in the field near Corpus Christi, some sixty acres of growing cabbage, all under irrigation. A few days after purchasing these crops, and while you were with the U. S. Weather Bureau at this point, you advised me one evening that a cold wave would reach Corpus Christi the following day, and advised me to flood my cabbage fields with water from our irrigation ditches. I immediately telephoned my men and had them flood the fields, as suggested, and as a result, the growing cabbage was very little damaged, although the thermometer went as low as seventeen degrees above zero, Fahrenheit, which was unusually cold for this section of the country.

"As a result of our saving our cabbage, it was sold at a good price, while cabbages growing in other fields that were not irrigated, suffered very severely from the freeze, and in a great many instances were entirely killed, thereby entailing a heavy loss upon the grower.

"I would have sustained the same loss in my crops had not you advised me promptly of the coming cold wave, and for this reason, we are warm advocates of the Government system of weather warnings.

"Wishing you success in your new field, and with best wishes, we are,

Very truly yours,
(Signed) C. E. Coleman."

Mr. C. H. Pease, a prominent citizen of Raymondville, Texas, who has used only crude-oil-burning heaters for the protection of orange trees, says:

"During the winter of 1911-12, I used heaters in a small orchard of oranges. The freeze on Thanksgiving was the first time I used them. The trees heated did not drop a leaf, while those adjoining that were not protected, lost all their leaves, and were frozen back. The second week in January, 1912, I again heated one night, with the result that the trees did not drop a leaf, while those not protected were frozen to the ground.

The protected trees bore lightly during the season of 1912, and in 1913 they bore heavily, yielding two boxes of excellent fruit to the tree. Those unprotected that froze to the ground came up, as they were banked with earth, and this year, 1914, they are also heavily loaded with fruit. The trees heated were planted thickly, about 200 to the acre. I used crude-oil burners, one pan to the tree. I had a thermometer in the center of one of the trees, and it never fell below 28 degrees during the night. No frost formed on the trees. Outside of protected area a thermometer registered 19 degrees, Fahrenheit. The night was calm (making it unusually favorable for this method of protection). With a high wind, I believe a windbreak, with wood fires on the north, would supplement the oil fires.

"Mr. M. L. Gilliland, of this place, covered an acre of watermelons with a conical frost protector and saved them from a late frost. From this acre, he loaded the first car of watermelons in this place and received $336, for the car load. He had some fifteen acres that were not protected and from them he sold $900 worth of melons. The acre protected yielded him about five times as much revenue per acre more than the land not covered.

"A large number of farmers are investing in these protectors, preparatory to planting watermelons early next spring.

Very truly yours,
(Signed)   C. H. Pease."

Mr. Marcus Philips, a leading citizen of Riviera, Texas, in writing of protection of citrus fruit trees, says:

"The forecasts of frost and freezing temperatures that I received from the U. S. Weather Bureau for several years, through you at Corpus Christi, Texas, were of great value as shown by the results of fruit trees protected.

"Citrus fruit trees at Riviera were protected by the use of canvas and a small lantern. The canvas was made like a wagon cover but long enough to reach around the tree, was drawn together at the top and bottom, and the lighted lantern placed inside at the base of the tree. This afforded absolute protection and did no damage. The lowest temperature recorded was 16 degrees F. on February 18, 1910.

"Citrus trees were also protected by covering with covered boxes and filling the space between the foliage and branches in the boxes with loose hay. This was also effective.

214   Supplement

"Nearly all the unprotected citrus trees during temperatures of 20 degrees or lower were severely injured or killed.

"Very little protection was given to vegetables in this locality. In a few instances watermelons and beets were plowed, drawing the dirt very close and almost covering the plants, which usually saved a large per cent of the crop."

The above article was written in 1914 at request of Chief U. S. Weather Bureau, Washington, D. C. It was published in the Monthly Weather Review, October, 1914, p. 591, under caption "Frost Protection by Irrigation in Southern Texas," by J. L. Cline, Weather Bureau, Dallas, Texas. It was also reprinted and published in full in a "Weather Bureau Supplement," printed by the U. S. Weather Bureau, Government Printing Office, Washington, D. C. And today this article is considered of great value to truck growers throughout the country.

WEATHER BUREAU WORK, INCLUDING SOME FEATURES OF THE AEROLOGICAL WORK OF THE BUREAU

By Joseph L. Cline, B.Sc.; A.M.; Ph.D. Year, 1935

I am glad to be with you today to convey to you some idea as to work performed by the U. S. Weather Bureau, an institution that records and keeps records of weather, which is one of the most talked-of subjects. And I hope I can give you a few thoughts of interest on one of the most important factors that go to make life possible on our "terrestrial globe."

Climate, or average run of weather, is one of the most important features of any country. It is nearly as important a part of the environment of animal life as it is of vegetable or plant existence. Some assert that climate outlines civilization, but we have not successfully proved this to be the case. However, soil can be changed artificially, without much expense, so as to be made very productive, if soil is all that is desired; but an unfavorable climate may be considered unchangeable, and will probably remain undesirable forever, though often some scientists declare, "Weather conditions are changing." Records covering long periods of time show that there have been changes, or fluctuations, with periods of hot and dry, and wet and cold weather, during all ages, and that a "perfect climate" does not exist; such conditions may be expected to continue through all time yet to come.

Texas, owing to its large area, topography, and geographical location, has a varied climate, partaking of the tropics in the south, and the temperate regions in the north, a circumstance which permits successful cultivation of about as many varieties of farm products as any other State in the United States. In some winters subfreezing temperatures have been noted in north Texas, while at the same time ripe strawberries were being harvested in the open fields on the Texas coast.

The climate of Texas is naturally affected by physical conditions and changes taking place in the atmosphere. With the approach of summer and the increase of solar heat in the northern hemisphere, there is a slight shifting northward in the movement of the high and low barometer areas as they cross the United States. The deflection of this movement to the northward of Texas during the summer months is favored by the surrounding topography, that is, the Rocky Mountains to the west, the plains country to the west and north, the great valleys to the eastward and the Gulf of Mexico to the south, together with the influence of the almost permanent summer low barometer area in Arizona. This northward movement is also accelerated by the inland temperatures in summer becoming higher than the temperatures over the large water area south of Texas. The distribution of pressure, temperature, and general conditions is such that the air flows northward almost constantly during the summer across Texas from the western part of the Gulf of Mexico. These southerly winds commence in March and last until October, and in midsummer reach the northern boundary of the United States along a strip of nearly 10 degrees of longitude, or about 500 miles wide, and 15 degrees of latitude, or about 1,000 miles long. These southerly winds (or southeasterly toward the central or western part of the State) bring coolness and comfort with them in the very season when coolness is most needed.

A marked characteristic, and a feature worthy of scientific investigation, is that dry periods of more or less intensity occur in some portions of Texas nearly every year, during the periods of the prevailing southerly winds. The drouthy periods generally start during the middle or latter part of June, but, in some years, damaging dry periods have not commenced until July. There appears never to have been a year in Texas when crops in some parts of the State were not affected during the growing season by drouth periods. There are dry periods in almost all agricultural sections of the world, when rain would improve the yield of growing crops, but they do not always come with the same regularity as the Texas summer drouths.

It is believed that weather and weather forecasting have been a subject for consideration almost since the creation of man; but the science of Meteorology was slow in developing accuracy and reliability, and the true value of this science is only now beginning to be fully appreciated by the general public. Recently Dr. Willis R. Gregg, now Chief U. S. Weather Bureau, stated:

"Roughly speaking, the world began to regard weather seriously about three quarters of a century ago. At that time agriculture, commerce, and marine navigation had been 'going concerns' for centuries. True, in more recent years, they have undergone marvelous development and change, but basically they were much the same then as now. It was necessary, therefore, that meteorological service be organized to meet the needs of these industries as they existed. With the change in all lines of industry that has since occurred, it has, of course, been necessary for meteorological service to adapt itself to these changes. The same factor that has played a major role in revolutionizing industry, namely, the marvelous development in the speed of communications, is likewise largely responsible for the changes that have taken place in weather service. Speed in assembling the data and promptness in making them and the forecasts based on them available for use are the all-essential features in providing service to all classes of industry. Fortunately, when aeronautics appeared on the scene, demanding its share of service, the proper tools were at hand. It was only necessary to sharpen some of them, reshape others, and put them all to work."

The Weather Bureau keeps continuous automatic records of atmospheric pressure, temperature, precipitation, wind velocity and direction, and sunshine, and observes and records thunderstorms, solar and lunar halos, and other optical phenomena. These records are available to the general public. Some business people use the Weather Bureau as though it were a part of their operating machinery. By an Act of Congress, Weather Bureau records are admissible in any court. Such records are often the deciding factor in many lawsuits. There are a few criminals now in the State penitentiary of Texas who would have been set free, had it not been for Weather Bureau records. I have had to take Weather Bureau records at Dallas, Texas, into the courts trying criminals at Fort Worth, Texas, so as to obtain conviction.

It is believed that Weather Bureau records at Dallas, Texas, are influential in the settlement of more contemplated lawsuits out of court than most large law firms settle in court. Let me offer an example of how the records are appreciated by those who use them. One day, not so long ago, a claim adjuster for a large company called at my office, looked over the Weather Bureau records, and, upon leaving, remarked, "If I go to court with those records against me, I will lose my suit, and I am going right now and compromise." Many lawyers study Weather Bureau records, then go and adjust their claims, and thereby save time and court costs.

Only a few years ago the aerological work of the Weather Bureau consisted of twice-daily pilot balloon observations at a few selected stations over the country, and kite ascents at five selected stations, carrying aloft an instrument recording pressure, temperature, humidity, and wind velocity. One of the aerological stations was at Groesbeck, Texas, which was closed when a central collecting airways control station was established under my jurisdiction at Love Field Airport, Dallas.

Duties of the Weather Bureau were materially increased with the inauguration of air mail, which required special weather service along the various air-mail routes. A pilot before a take-off desires to know wind velocities and direction, weather conditions aloft, weather conditions along his route, and what weather changes will occur between the time he leaves and the time he will arrive at his destination. To meet this demand, frequent and regular weather reporting stations were established along the various air-mail routes, with an occasional reporting off-line station, so as to furnish reports to the central control stations for use in making and disseminating four-hourly forecasts, and giving weather conditions along the flying routes, solely for airways service, which is a separate and different service from that rendered by the regular Weather Bureau stations or City Offices.

Reports as now made, transmitted, and broadcasted for airways service, contain ceiling, sky conditions, visibility, temperature, dew point, wind direction and velocity, barometric pressure and pertinent remarks as to weather conditions. These reports are made hourly over routes equipped with teletype, or radio facilities, and less frequently for scheduled departures of airplanes over other routes; the teletype and radio facilities are available over most traveled air routes. Airways forecasts are statements of expected conditions as to weather, ceiling, and visibility along air routes. The term "weather," in airways forecasts, means cloudiness, precipitation, fog, thunderstorms, icing conditions, squalls, and the like.

Pilot balloon observations are made at Love Field Airport and certain other airway stations from two to four times daily. Equipment for making pilot balloon reports consists of a small six-inch rubber balloon, inflated with hydrogen gas to about 27 inches, and having a definite free-lift of 140 grams. This definite free-lift gives the balloon, when released, a constant ascensional rate of 180 meters (about 600 feet) a minute. The balloon as it ascends is observed through a theodolite. Readings are made of the elevation and azimuth angles of the balloon every minute, and are usually transmitted over a short-line telephone to another employee in the office, who computes the horizontal distance of the balloon from the station at each minute interval, and plots this information on a large circular, celluloid protractor. In this manner the direction and velocity at any altitude can be determined. These balloons are very often watched up into the stratosphere before they burst, or disappear because of the horizontal distance from the observer or their passage off into clouds. They have been observed over ten miles high and fifteen miles away.

The Weather Bureau started to make observations of temperature, pressure, and humidity aloft by airplane at Dallas, Texas, under my supervision, on July 1, 1931, which was an improvement over the kite method used at Groesbeck, Texas, and other meteorological stations. The flights by airplane are made daily at 4 a. m., 90th meridian time, or as soon thereafter as possible when weather conditions prevent the regular flight. As an example of regularity of the airplane observations, on only two days since July 1, 1931, have observations been missed on account of unfavorable weather. The altitude reached by these flights, except for a few observations when icing conditions or motor trouble prevented, has been very close to 17,000 feet above the ground.

For making observations aloft, a simple instrument recording pressure, temperature, and humidity, known as an aerometeorograph and weighing about seven pounds, is used, suspended from some part of the airplane by means of shock cords to eliminate vibration, and in such a position as to eliminate dynamic pressure effects and temperature effect due to heat of the motor. On a biplane, as is used at Dallas, Texas, the aerometeorograph is suspended between the two wings, and far enough out from the fuselage to be out of the propeller blast. Every precaution is used against erroneous records. The aerometeorographs are calibrated every three months, and are not used until the calibrations have been approved by the Aerological Division officials at Washington D. C. The accuracy of the instruments is such that it is not at all uncommon for one test to show the same results as did a previous test.

Under the old kite method of making upper-air observations, if winds were favorable and observations started at 7 a. m. C. S. T. it would sometimes be afternoon before the data obtained could be transmitted to forecast centers; but, with present methods of using the airplane, the results of the ascents are in the hands of the various forecast centers before the morning forecasts are issued.

At the present time, airplane observations are being made by the Weather Bureau at Dallas, Texas; Omaha, Nebraska; Pembina, North Dakota, and Cleveland, Ohio; by the U. S. Navy at Pensacola, Florida; Norfolk, Va.; Washington, D. C.;

San Diego, California, and Seattle, Washington; and by the Massachusetts Institute of Technology, at Boston, Massachusetts.

With the ever-increasing knowledge of the science of Meteorology and the research studies in forecasting, there has been an increasing demand for observations as to the vertical structure of the atmosphere as well as to the horizontal structure. Such studies are being carried on in almost all of the more advanced countries having a meteorological service.

Sounding balloon observations were made during the Polar Year 1932-1933. Large rubber balloons inflated with hydrogen gas were released at Love Field Airport, Dallas, Texas, and at other selected points over the world, carrying aloft a small meteorograph weighing about seven ounces and recording pressure, temperature, and humidity. This type of equipment is intended to penetrate the stratosphere. The balloon is free and, when it bursts, a releasing device allows the meteorograph to float to earth on a small parachute. A reward is offered to the finder as an inducement for the safe return of the instrument with its record to the releasing point. Most of the instruments released at Love Field Airport, Dallas, Texas, were found and returned; and all returned generally had readable records.

One man plowing near Carrollton, Texas, found one of the meteorographs and, while he was bringing it to Dallas to get his reward, his brother found another one near by and brought it in and received his reward for it. One of the meteorographs was found in a tree in Arkansas by two colored men; they heard the clock ticking and thought it was a rattlesnake. They went to a white man's house to get a gun to shoot it. The white man took his gun and went with them, and, as he had read about the balloon ascensions, he knew it was a meteorograph, recovered it, returned it to Love Field, and received the reward.

The foregoing address on Weather Bureau work was written and delivered in 1935. There has been little improvement in the Weather Bureau since then up to the present year, 1943. General Weather Service has been consolidated with Airways Service and has been moved from city offices, at many of the larger points, to airports

As a result, the public has not been receiving as effective weather service as formerly, when it had city offices dealing with "general weather" only. The cost of operating the airways service is now more than four times the amount formerly required for doing the same job, and the sole marked improvement achieved is an increase in the number of reports and a more rapid system of obtaining observations of upper air currents. Despite the greater expenditure, services rendered by the U. S. Weather Bureau during the past eight years have been of such quality that the U. S. Army, the U. S. Navy and the large airlines have set up independent weather services for their own use in order to obtain more efficient weather data. When the Weather Bureau was first established, it was placed in the U. S. Army Signal Corps, and many believe that it should be transferred back to the Army, where it is most needed today.

Weather forecasting never, it is likely, will be absolutely perfect, but remember this: it is better always to go by Weather Bureau warnings and be prepared, should the conditions predicted come to pass, than to fail to heed warnings given and so lose property and perhaps even life.

It is believed that some improvement in weather forecasting can be accomplished if forecasters will pay less attention to cold and warm "fronts," will make closer study of weather conditions behind the "fronts," and will note the character of weather which occurs in different localities over the country with the passing of the various types of such "fronts."

Records of general weather service should be kept up to date, as such records show the kind of conditions likely to occur in the future for the various seasons of the year, in all parts of the world. Such information is of great value to commerce, and is of much greater value in time of wars in enabling strategists to determine in advance the ideal periods in which important battles may be staged.

In closing let me say, "the world is all right, just as God made it to be". But rulers and the people of all nations are to blame for the present undesirable and deplorable conditions. Let us hope and pray that future generations will always elect honest rulers, and that the new rulers, and the people as a mass, will have one motto, "be honest, live and let live", so as to make a just and happy world. Then there will be no "global wars", and this old world of ours will be a much better place in which to live.

9 781565 547834